STUPID  ELEPHANT  TRICKS

"Of two evils, choose neither."

~ Charles Haddon Spurgeon

STUPID ELEPHANT TRICKS

BY SCOTT ALAN BUSS

For my Brothers and Sisters who love America, liberty, freedom, and the pursuit of excellence, all completely by God's grace and explicitly for His glory.

R3PENTANCE **R3VIVAL** **R3VOLUTION**

www.R3VOLUTIONPRESS.com

CONTENTS

CONTENTS
CONTINUED

CONFESSIONS OF A STUPID ELEPHANT
THE REPENTANCE AND REFORMATION OF A CHRISTIAN CONSERVATIVE

> *...what partnership has righteousness with lawlessness? Or what fellowship has light with darkness? What accord has Christ with Belial? Or what portion does a believer share with an unbeliever? What agreement has the temple of God with idols? For we are the temple of the living God...*
>
> 2 CORINTHIANS 6:14-16

> "Of two evils, choose neither."
>
> CHARLES HADDON SPURGEON

Is my vote honoring to my God? This is the question that, by His grace alone, I've aimed to sincerely ask and honestly contemplate, and the serious consideration of this question is what I hope and pray to inspire in all other American Christians through this book.

As a thankful child of the '80s, I have a soft spot and deep admiration for Ronald Reagan and what God chose to do through him for America in what was truly a desperate, dark time in the nation's history. As a politically inclined young man in the '90s, I also have something of a soft spot for Rush Limbaugh and the radio revolution he began "back in the day" of George H.W. Bush's "kinder, gentler nation". (I even refused to purchase the text book for a college sociology class taught by a gay ("homosexual", not "happy") Marxist, instead opting to carry a copy of Rush's *The Way Things Ought to Be* with me to class every day.) And as a vocal supporter of the younger Bush's campaigns in the decade that followed his father's presidency, I have a very warm affection for good ol' red state, Tea Party patriotism and sensibility.

None of these things have changed.

I love America. I love her Constitution. I love her history. I love her unique wonder and witness to the providential hand and power of God. I love her role and influence in a dark world insofar as she has been able to attain and sustain that biblical "shining city on a hill" position mentioned so frequently and so fondly by President Reagan.

I love conservative books, I love talk radio, and I love the fact that God has given American Christians all of these things along with the power and opportunity to use them to shape our own government - something that is breathtakingly rare in human history. I love that we have no Caesar in America (at least not yet). I love that *We the People* are Caesar (at least for now).

But each of these loves have been, for me, cast in a new light. By the grace of God alone, I've only recently been granted enough light and the desire to face it so that I might come to see and contemplate that question differently. More seriously. More urgently. More *faithfully.*

Is my vote honoring to my God?

Considering what I have been graced to learn and live through His perfect Word, *is my vote honoring to my God?* Knowing what I have been blessed to see and understand about His nature and necessity as the center of all hopeful human endeavor, *is my vote honoring to my God?* Having embraced the truth that He has given me through His written revelations regarding the need to exalt and submit to Him in all things at all times, even (and especially) when doing so is decidedly unpopular and non-pragmatic by every self-serving standard and worldly impulse, *is my vote honoring to my God?*

As I first began to seriously contemplate this question a few short years ago, I immediately realized that repentance was required. And in that same moment I also realized what it was that had played such a large part in my having previously avoided the true weight of the question altogether: **Pride.**

It was anything but comfortable to realize that *I* had been so far off the mark. And it was hardly a warm and fuzzy feeling that washed over me at the realization that I had been that far off the mark when I had, all along, had my God's *perfect* truth plainly preserved and presented before me the whole time.

It wasn't as though Scripture was vague, cloudy, or ambiguous regarding such vital truths as the centrality and lordship of Christ in all things at all times. It wasn't exactly wishy-washy as to the price of submitting to Christ in each and every one of those things, either. And it sure wasn't the least little bit wobbly or wiggle-room-friendly as to how counter-intuitive and downright peculiar the Christian life in action would appear from a worldly perspective. God's Word couldn't have been clearer on any of these things. It was as though it was perfect or something....and that perfection was cutting through a lot of pet positions, perspectives, and traditions that I'd *proudly* held close and dear for a very long time.

I realized that I had been *very* secularly pragmatic in my political thoughts and actions. I had been *very* self-focused, self-referential, and self-centered in my political thoughts and actions. And I had been all of these things in spite of my having known better all along.

Now here I am, in the year of our Lord 2012, and I see an America that is circling the drain in every significant, measurable way. Realizing that it is doing so in no small part due to the choices that *I* have made, the causes that *I* have supported, and the candidates for whom *I* have voted has not exactly proven to be my idea of a good time. It really was much more fun when I could just blame those evil and/or stupid Democrats for everything.

But the course that's been charted for America isn't an exclusively Democrat construct. Far from it. It isn't a Republican

3

creation, either. It is the product of a *progressivism* that has captivated both parties, and the "progress" at the heart of both its right wing and left wing variants is a progress toward a man-centered worldview and away from a God-centered one. If this path is followed for just a little while longer, we really will see the doom that has been waiting for us since we started down this trail.

I love America. I love God more than America. Infinitely more.

So it is that I love America enough to root for her when she seeks and submits to His will, I love her enough to root against her when she goes the other way, and I love her enough to fight for her shifting to the former path when she is presently choosing the latter. My fidelity is, happily and adoringly, to God above all else, and that is the prism through which, by His grace, I aim to test all things - including all *political* things - and then ask the question: *Is my vote honoring to my God?*

My prayer is that the hard truths and bold statements made in the pages of *Stupid Elephant Tricks* will be understood with four keys kept on hand and in mind:

1. **This book is written primarily to Christians.** There is a roughly zero percent chance that much of what's written in these pages will even begin to make sense to anyone else. That said, it is hoped that the Gospel presentation contained in these pages might be used by the Lord to add to His church as He sees fit. He is trusted *completely* in this regard.

2. **All that any of us have - including any bit of knowledge or wisdom or insight - is a gift from God.** None of us have any room to boast in ourselves, though we can and should boast in the Lord who has given us all of these things. I certainly do not imagine for a moment that I am inherently any better than any of those whom I may criticize herein. I am not. Of all the people I've ever met or heard of or even read about in a history book, the one of whom I am most aware as a sinful, selfish person is: Me.

By God's grace, He has saved me, and by His grace He is sanctifying me, but based on what I know about my own heart and my own mind, I do not for a single solitary second seriously present myself as inherently better than *anyone*.

3. **This book does not pretend to represent or aspire to become a benchmark or standard setter for Christian political thought.** The Bible *is* that book. This one is just an imperfect set of observations written by an imperfect man who hopes and prays that God will choose to graciously use these clumsy words and expressions to draw His people toward Him as the source of every meaningful bit of knowledge. I am not proposing or implying or even close to implying that those who arrive at different conclusions than I express on the subjects covered herein are in any way, as a result of such a difference, demonstrating that they are not "real" Christians or that they are in any way less of a Christian. The Bible is their proving ground for such things; this book is not.

4. **We must seek biblical answers to every question - including the political.** The whole thrust of this book is aimed at simply inspiring Christians to cast every political question in the perfect light of Scripture and then submit to what is revealed in that light - no matter the cost in this fleeting, temporal world.

So have grace towards others - including me and every target of criticism noted in these pages. Love as you have been loved. And then stand for the truth as the Lover of your soul has commanded, with all boldness and confidence in Him.

I trust that He will guide us all along the way as we take this journey together. He has placed us purposefully in such a time and place and situation as this. That reality is both a matchless comfort and a magnificently daunting challenge. And we shouldn't want it any other way.

We have a nation to save, but we have a God to honor first. May He never again allow us to forget this. Thank you for your patience, grace, and desire to pursue His truth in all things.

Soli Deo Gloria...and let's roll!

SAB

March 25, 2012

SECTION ONE

~

Starting the Forbidden Conversation

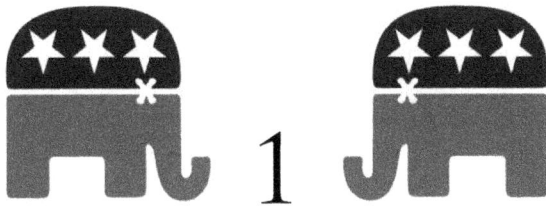

WHY SETTLE FOR THE LESSER EVIL?
THE SLAVERY AND STUPIDITY OF SECULAR STANDARDS

"No candidate should become the spokesman for his faith, for if he becomes President, he will need the prayers of the people of all faiths. [Loud applause] **I believe that every faith that I've encountered draws its adherents closer to god.**"[1]

MITT ROMNEY
(BOLD EMPHASIS ADDED)

"Evil will always triumph, because good is dumb."

DARK HELMET, *SPACEBALLS*

"Why Settle for the *Lesser* Evil?"

Now there's a campaign slogan you don't see every day, at least not yet. But there it was, all decked out in red, white, and blue; proudly planted on the bobbing back bumper of the little Nissan

---

[1] Politico, 12.14.11 - http://www.politico.com/news/stories/1211/70416.html)

9

pickup in front of me. "Cthulhu for President" was the headlining banner above the peculiarly provocative tagline.

Cthulhu (pronounced: kuh-THOO-loo...I think), for those of you (no doubt happily) unaware of the name, is the moniker given to a dark, malevolent force of supernatural terror in a series of horror stories first penned by H.P. Lovecraft back in the late '20s. Often described along the lines of "...an octopus, a dragon, and a human caricature.... A pulpy, tentacled head surmounted a grotesque scaly body with rudimentary wings"[2], Mr. Cthulhu certainly had the look to go with the bad attitude and mission.

Somewhere between his intro in 1928 and the 2000 presidential campaign, enthusiastic Lovecraft and/or Cthulhu fans took (what can only be hoped to be) a tongue-in-cheek approach to the "pulpy, tentacle headed" doom-bringer in question and did what Americans do so well so naturally: They happily (and profitably) took on the mission of marketing their favorite force of darkness in every way imaginable and then some.

There were "funny" Cthulhu t-shirts. There were tasty Cthulhu candies. There were even adorable(?) little Cthulhu Beanie Baby style plushies. And then there was the ongoing "presidential campaign", with shirts, slogans, and...bumper stickers. Bumper stickers like the one rolling along ahead of me a few cycles back.

While I've not bothered to check on the latest incarnation of Cthulhu for President in the present election cycle, one can only assume that he and his handlers are at it again, and happily so. Whatever terrible thing that may or may not say about our culture's condition, now, more than ever, the "Why Settle for the *Lesser Evil?*" line seems worthy of serious consideration, even if its tentacle-headed advocate does not.

Incredibly, sadly, and incredibly sadly, professing Christians in America have not only managed to validate at least a substantial portion of something as idiotic as the Cthulhu campaign for high office, they have also managed to confirm the strategic observations of another pop-culture bad guy wannabe. When the Dark Helmet character (a Darth Vader knock-off) in Mel Brook's

---

[2] H.P. Lovecraft, *The Call of Cthulhu*

Spaceballs flick (a *Star Wars* knock-off) announced confidently that, "Evil will always triumph, because good is dumb.", he hit the nail on the head...so long as "good" is described by secular standards...which is *exactly* how most politically active professing Christians define it in practice these days. It is this shift toward secular pragmatism and secular standards of goodness in American Christendom that has made the question "Why settle for the lesser evil?" so sadly relevant today.

In agreeing to measure the goodness or rightness of anything, much less the political leadership of our nation, by any standard other than God's, we have made a compelling case for "choosing the lesser evil" and have, in doing so, proven that our "good" is, in fact, dumb. Frighteningly dumb. As Christians, we are *supposed* to know and advocate *explicitly* God-centered goodness as the only true sort of goodness to be found, but, in practice - particularly political practice - we simply do not believe this to be true.

We. Are. Dumb.

And unlike the kind of dumb that you *might* be able to laugh at in *Spaceballs* or a Cthulhu presidential campaign (not that I necessarily recommend either, mind you), ours is a form of willful stupidity that is far more dangerous and far more destructive, in part because it is God's own people who are often perpetuating this decidedly *un*godly approach to life in *His* name.

We've become "politically savvy" Christians who know how to play the game to win! And just look at all of the "winning" we've experienced with this approach: We murder roughly a million innocent children each year, mostly for convenience; we tax young workers to support the Ponzi scheme of all Ponzi schemes in the form of ever expanding and long-known-to-be-unsustainable entitlement programs; we are on the cusp of formally exalting homosexuality - *which God hates* - as a legitimate and honorable "lifestyle", and we are witnessing at this very moment our comically unbiblical and unconstitutional statist system make its final, lumbering lunge toward much more formally tyrannical approaches in every realm given up to its dominion.

And many of these progressive wonders have been won by *us* in *His* name as we have done everything we can see (and have been told) to do by the forces of secularly defined progress within conservative, libertarian, and Republican political circles. Where once we would at least pretend to seek God enough to insist that our candidates profess to be actual, orthodox Christians, we now find that to be more than negotiable.

After all, we have to *win*, right? We *must* beat Obama! That is our supreme goal...our ultimate challenge...our clear and present *idol*.

It is this idol, in various incarnations, that has been used very effectively and for a very long time by the enemy. In our embrace of this idol, we have abandoned our duty to truth and its Author and we have surrendered our one and only supernatural hope of actually winning "the culture war" or any other conflict of consequence. In agreeing with a godless culture that God is not the necessary explicit center for *all* good things, we have joined, in a very real sense, something even worse the "Cthulhu for President" campaign.

American Christians now fiercely believe and vigorously campaign for the "lesser" evil, and, in doing so, we do exactly that for which the greatest evil hopes. After all, if it's not hard to imagine how pleased a Cthulhu or a Dark Helmet type might be at the prospect of directing his enemy's future by simply presenting multiple evils from which that supposed "good guy" preemptively agrees to choose, then how much more so should we understand the very *real* delight of Satan at the prospect of manipulating America's professing Christians in precisely the same manner?

Apparently, all the devil need do is hold out an Obama or a Clinton or a Carter in his left hand whenever he desires for American Christians to select whatever and whomever he chooses to offer up in his right. And professing Christians in America have, for quite some time now, been all too happy to play along. We just seem to love dancing to the "less evil" tune, no matter how obviously unbiblical it is or how much wreckage accumulates in its ever-lengthening, ever-widening, and ever-deepening wake.

The Christian response to the political question, "Why choose the lesser evil?" should *not* be an explanation as to why said lesser evil should be chosen. The Christian response to this biblically ridiculous question should be something along the lines of:

Why choose *any* evil?

Or, as Charles Spurgeon famously and wisely recommended: "Of two evils, choose neither."

Those of us who are Christians have been bought with a price. We are *His* slaves where once we were slaves to sin. Our breaths, our heartbeats, our actions *and our votes* are *His* property. We will answer to Him for how we spend every one of them.

This is the blessed reality that should inform our every thought and action, and this is the only hope that we have as we consider our calling and placement in a culture so vividly aligned with that described in the book of Romans:

> *For **the wrath of God is revealed from heaven against all ungodliness and unrighteousness of men, who by their unrighteousness suppress the truth**. For what can be known about God is plain to them, because God has shown it to them. For his invisible attributes, namely, his eternal power and divine nature, have been clearly perceived, ever since the creation of the world, in the things that have been made. So they are without excuse. For although they knew God, they did not honor him as God or give thanks to him, but they became futile in their thinking, and their foolish hearts were darkened. Claiming to be wise, they became fools, and exchanged the glory of the immortal God for images resembling mortal man and birds and animals and creeping things.*
>
> *Therefore **God gave them up in the lusts of their hearts to impurity, to the dishonoring of their bodies among themselves, because they exchanged the truth about God for a lie and worshiped and served the***

creature rather than the Creator, who is blessed forever! Amen.

*For this reason **God gave them up to dishonorable passions.** **For their women exchanged natural relations for those that are contrary to nature; and the men likewise gave up natural relations with women and were consumed with passion for one another, men committing shameless acts with men and receiving in themselves the due penalty for their error.***

*And since they did not see fit to acknowledge God, **God gave them up to a debased mind to do what ought not to be done.** They were filled with all manner of unrighteousness, evil, covetousness, malice. They are full of envy, murder, strife, deceit, maliciousness. They are gossips, slanderers, haters of God, insolent, haughty, boastful, inventors of evil, disobedient to parents, foolish, faithless, heartless, ruthless. **Though they know God's righteous decree that those who practice such things deserve to die, they not only do them but give approval to those who practice them.** [3]*

In response to such clear and present realities, we will often see and hear our brothers and sisters in Christ cite promises and verses from elsewhere in the Word, including, quite frequently, the matchlessly comforting and inspiring words of 2 Chronicles 7:14:

*if my people who are called by my name **humble themselves,** and pray and seek my face and turn from their wicked ways, then I will hear from heaven and will forgive their sin and heal their land.*

---

[3] Romans 1:18-32

But what if the God who has made this perfect promise has also clearly defined the humility mentioned in the passage? What if He has made plain that *we are to be humble by submitting to His will completely*? What if He has also made plain that anything less than complete submission to Him in such a manner is not humility at all, no matter how much we might like to imagine or spin or pretend otherwise. What if He has lovingly warned His children that failure to submit to His clearly revealed will *is always the precise opposite of God-glorifying personal humility*. It is always God-hating, self-centered *pride*.

Pride is the fuel of all man-centered pragmatism, and man-centered pragmatism has most certainly come to define, in many ways and on every front, the prevailing political attitudes of the vast majority of professing Christians in America.

But take heart!

There is hope.

Perfect hope.

Supernatural hope.

But do we want that hope? Will we humble ourselves as *He* defines humility and requires it of His people?

Or will we continue to pragmatically play the game and dance to the tune that His enemy (and ours) has so happily arranged and offered up to us? Will we work and fight and pray for the sock puppet on the right simply because he is soooooo much "less evil" than the one on the left? Or will we finally come to the place of agreement with Scripture and Spurgeon, who both exhort, "Of two evils, choose neither."

While Cthulhu is a fiction, the perils of this age are anything but. In the hills of modern progressive America, there be dragons...*real* dragons...home grown, pragmatically nurtured, and ultimately lethal creatures bent on the pursuit of anything and everything *but* the explicit will of God...all in the name of progress, of course.

Our only real hope to slay these dragons lies on the other side of our proper understanding and *application* of what He describes as "the Sword of Truth" - His perfect Word.

What if the whole key to the nightmare situation in which we have placed ourselves really is simple, complete *submission* to God, as He has defined it so lovingly and so clearly in His Word? The belief that this is indeed the case will be a guiding principle of this book, and the encouragement of fellow believers to pursue that calling will be a central goal.

When we are led, by His grace, to submit to Him completely as *He* has commanded us to do - and only when we do so - all truly good things really do become possible. Only through the supernaturally inspired and inspiring submission that He has provided can we actually claim otherwise unimaginable and impossible victories throughout the American cultural landscape...one slain dragon and one saved person at a time.

So man up, grab your Sword, seek and submit to *His* will in *all* things, and prep for a *real* fight! No evil is to be spared; lesser, greater, or any in-between. The hunt is on.

2

POLITICS, RELIGION, AND THE THREAT OF SPONTANEOUS COMBUSTION

AN INTRO TO TACKLING STUPID ELEPHANT TRICKS

And Jesus came and said to them, "All authority in heaven and on earth has been given to me. Go therefore and make disciples of all nations, baptizing them in the name of the Father and of the Son and of the Holy Spirit, teaching them to observe all that I have commanded you. And behold, I am with you always, to the end of the age."

MATTHEW 28:18-20

"Duty is ours; consequences are God's."

JOHN JAY

Remember when all the really bad hypotheticals were still hypotheticals? Ah, those were the good ol' days...days when America was merely *on the verge of* moral implosion, *heading toward* the brink of socio-economic collapse, and so on. Now we're there. We *have* imploded morally and we *are* on the brink of total socio-economic darkness. The really bad hypotheticals of justa generation past - at least most of them - aren't hypothetical anymore. They're a part of recent history and the present.

One of the saddest realities in all of this is that we don't even seem to much question the inevitability of our own doom anymore. We just sort of assume it's coming and try to make the best of things 'til it arrives to finish us off. The trajectory has been so bad for so long that it just *is*. The unspoken motivation for our relative silence and inaction tends to be that we simply do not believe that there's anything that can actually be done about it - at least not in a way that has the truly world-shaking power or permanence needed to qualify as a real solution. We no longer believe that the tide can be turned, and, hand in glove with the sad embrace of that suicide-by-autopilot concession has come the sorry notion that the best we can hope for is the pragmatic preservation of as much personal comfort as we can muster 'til the end finally comes.

As Christians, we are most to blame for this. We know better; at least we *should* know better. We are the salt. We are the light. And where America has lost her way, we are most to blame.

It is in the context of our uniquely *American* setting - living in the United States and knowing, even now, so many of its blessings - that we find ourselves even more responsible for what we see (and so often complain about) happening all around us. We have been given so much - freedoms and liberties the likes of which were unthinkable for the vast majority of people ever born, and as we have neglected our responsibility to keep those freedoms in the one and only perfect light of His truth, we have escorted them along the way to their slow demise and are about to witness their formal burial.

Rome is burning, alright. And *we* lit the fire.

But whatever you do, don't stop to notice. And whatever you do after noticing (which you weren't supposed to do in the first place, remember?), don't go talking about what you weren't supposed to notice with anyone else. Just shut up, snap those blinders back in place, and move along..."there's nothing to see here."

Silence is golden. Silence is precious. Silence is key; the key to maintaining and expanding all of the wonderful "progress" thathas been changing the face and foundation of America for around 100 years now, and with the endgame so near after so much hard work, we just need to keep our minds and mouths shut for a little bit longer. One by one, the realms we've surrendered to secular supervision have fallen, and fallen hard...all by design. Family...church...economy...community...art...literature...business...*po litics*...

We lit the fire of our freedom's end when we bought into the lie that *any* realm of thought or action should - or *could* - be kept safely sequestered from being subjected to the lordship of Jesus Christ and that anything good would then come of it.

Where Christians once drove the most important conversations by posing the most important questions and providing the most important answers, we have now largely abandoned our once beautiful, bold, up-stream struggle for His truth. In doing so, we have lost the life that comes only through that truth and its vigorous defense.

The defense of God's truth is a life-long process, one meaning of which is that when a people stop vigorously defending that truth, they stop truly living. They die. And where America was once a nation shaped most by those who loved, lived, and defended the most beautiful, deep, and challenging truths of Scripture, we have now allowed her to be shaped by those with the least knowledge of Scripture and the lowest regard for its value. More often than not, we've voted such people into power...*enthusiastically*.

If we are to return to the truth that frees fallen men and again know the liberty for which America was once, long ago known, we must first return to the one and only source of true liberty, true freedom, and true light: God. God above all else in all things and at all times. The explicitly God-centered path is our only hope, and our way back to that path will require our once again inspiring those most important conversations through our asking the most important questions and providing the most important answers.

That's what Christians used to do around here. Lord willing, that is what we will do again.

A QUESTION OF FREEDOM AND THE FREEDOM TO QUESTION

It is the responsibility of princes to know the extent of their authority **and of subjects to know to what extent they may obey princes**

JUNIUS BRUTUS, *A DEFENCE OF LIBERTY AGAINST TYRANTS*
(BOLD EMPHASIS ADDED)

Tell us, then, what you think. Is it lawful to pay taxes to Caesar, or not?" But Jesus, aware of their malice, said, "Why put me to the test, you hypocrites? Show me the coin for the tax." And they brought him a denarius. And Jesus said to them, "Whose likeness and inscription is this?" They said, "Caesar's." Then he said to them, "Therefore render to Caesar the things that are Caesar's, **and to God the things that are God's.**"

MATTHEW 22:17-21
(BOLD EMPHASIS ADDED)

Who *owns* marriage?

Who is the Author of life and has commanded the protection of innocents? Who is the Author of true liberty? True freedom?

When must we resist or oppose secular leadership that resists or opposes the Author of life and liberty in matters of life and liberty?

These are the questions that we must ask, first of ourselves (as we then look to the perfect Word of God for the answers), and then

20

of those in the sinking world around us so that we might, by His grace and for His glory, inspire and guide them to the same light that has provided our salvation and inspired our conviction.

It is out of our love for our Lord and our fidelity to His beautiful truth that we should ask questions like, "When are we obligated to obey secular authorities, and when, if ever, are we not only able to rightly disobey them, but obligated to do so?" and "Is it lawful to resist a secular ruler who actively resists God's Word and Church?"

If questions like this make you squirm, you are not alone. They have never been popular because they have never been easy. Yet, by God's grace, these are precisely the sorts of thoughts and questions that fueled the Christ-centered perspectives that formed the spearhead of the American Revolution and founding of the United States.

Long before Thomas Paine and his secularly-rooted *Common Sense* hit the scene, there was a work that played a major role in sharpening the understanding of Christians in America in the years leading up to the war for her independence and the founding of what was, for all of its monumental (and mounting) weaknesses, far and away, the greatest nation that this world has ever seen.

In their exposure to *A Defence of Liberty Against Tyrants*, first published in 1579, the American colonial Christian was encouraged to ask such currently unthinkable questions as those posed above. It was the recognition of a biblical basis for opposing tyranny that propelled this work to great popularity in pre-Revolution America and helped greatly to make possible the reality of a post-Revolution United States.

TYRANTS, KINGS, AND *THE* KING

The tyrant would pretend to be what the true king is.
Knowing that men are wonderfully attracted to and
enamoured of virtue, he endeavors with much subtlety
to make his vices appear yet masked with some shadow
of virtue. But let him counterfeit ever so cunningly; the
fox will still be known by his tail; and although he
fawn and flatter like a spaniel, yet his snarling and
grinning will always betray his currish kind.

> JUNIUS BRUTUS, *A DEFENCE OF*
> *LIBERTY AGAINST TYRANTS*
> (BOLD EMPHASIS ADDED)

Ever wondered *why*?

More specifically, why Christians supported the American revolution; a rebellion against their king?

Many answers are there to be found, if only we will look, though sometimes it seems as though we'd rather not, lest we fall under the same sense of obligation that must have swept over our founders "back in the day". We don't tend to want anything like that - an obligation that would shake our world so profoundly and require so much of us when we'd really just much rather take...it...*easy.*

Easy is what we do.

We're Americans. We're lazy, fat, and (at least pretend to be) happy about it.

And that must change.

One helpful ingredient in promoting that change is an examination of elements from Junius Brutus' *A Defence of Liberty Against Tyrants*, a work built around four vital, thought-provoking questions:

1. Are Subjects required or even obligated to obey Princes if they command that which is against the Law of God?

2. Is it lawful to resist a Prince who actively (or only passively) resist's God's Word and His Church?

3. Is it lawful to resist a Prince who actively (or only passively) works to destroy the civil order and to what extent may the resistance be made?

4. Are Princes permitted or required by God's Law to give aid to the subjects of another Prince, if those people are afflicted because of their Christian faith or oppressed by obvious tyranny?

These are the questions that colonial American Christians were asking in the time leading up to the American Revolution. And the answers - the *biblical* answers - that they found to these questions were, in large part, what fueled their enthusiastic participation in the American Revolution.

We will be revisiting these long forgotten questions of *A Defence of Liberty Against Tyrants* here, and will aim to test modern American (and particularly Republican) ideas, ideals and leadership in light of the principles contained and advocated therein, but as the main thrust of this book is to inspire the serious, sincere pursuit of truth through the asking and contemplation of powerful questions such as these, we will be frequently dwelling on the mere necessity and beauty of the questions themselves.

The beauty of these questions and the truth-seeking, God-centered views that motivated their pursuit at the dawn of our nation's history is something that's been far too obscured for far too long.

When we are finally willing and able to, by God's grace, ask these sorts of questions and seek their honest, accurate answers, no matter how challenging or hard those answers may be, we will have taken an early step toward a God-centered, God-glorifying path to true liberty's defense...and we will finally be ready to have true, good, and godly patriotic conversations; the kinds of conversations that inspire all of the best, God-centered pursuits...and all of the best, God-centered revolutions.

OBEYING THE KING OF KINGS IN ALL THINGS

*Let every person be subject to the governing authorities. For **there is no authority except from God**, and those that exist have been instituted by God. Therefore whoever resists the authorities resists what God has appointed, and those who resist will incur judgment. For **rulers are not a terror to good conduct, but to bad.** Would you have no fear of the one who is in authority? Then do what is good, and you will receive his approval, for he is God's servant for your good. But if you do wrong, be afraid, for he does not bear the sword in vain. For he is the servant of God, an avenger who carries out God's wrath on the wrongdoer. **Therefore one must be in subjection, not only to avoid God's wrath but also for the sake of conscience.***

ROMANS 13:1-5
(BOLD EMPHASIS ADDED)

*If God commands one thing, and the king commands
the contrary, who is that proud man that would term
him a rebel who refuses to obey the king, when it
means he must disobey God?* **But he should be
condemned and held as truly rebellious who does not
obey God, or who obeys the king when he forbids him
to yield obedience to God.**

JUNIUS BRUTUS, *A DEFENCE OF
LIBERTY AGAINST TYRANTS*
(BOLD EMPHASIS ADDED)

As we ramp up and prepare to roll into these good questions and
conversations, maintaining a God-centered perspective is essential.
When we consider a thing - *any*thing - our first and guiding goal
should always be to discover and embrace the will of God.

This is our prize: To know and conform to the will of our Lord,
wherever His truth takes us. However secularly non-pragmatic or
unpopular or unreasonable the revealed will of God may be (and it
will be all of these things to the world) we are to go there to the
embrace of His truth and stand upon it, whatever the price.

What is a tyrant? What is tyranny? What is a Christian's role in
the opposition of tyranny and the defense of liberty? What is
reasonable economic policy and what is the role of the state?

These are the questions that we must grow comfortable in asking,
and the answers to these questions are to be openly (meaning,
publically, whenever possible) sought first in the perfect, sufficient
Word of God. Our comfort will grow into boldness in the best
sense when we saturate our minds in the Word and grow in the
otherwise impossible combination of personal humility and
boldness in Christ that comes through the supernatural power of
Scripture surging through the life of an obedient believer.

Yet even as we earnestly pursue this path of God-centered
political contemplation through the study and application of His
Word in our lives, we must remain vigilant in our defense against

the many all-too-common and all-too-comfortable inclinations of our fallen and often silly little selves, including:

1. **The desire to pursue God's truth <u>first</u> for America's sake, or the economy's sake, or the culture's sake, or even for our own family's sake.** Each of these motivations, when they are primary in position, are plainly wrong, and must be acknowledged as such. The exaltation of any otherwise "good thing" above God is always sin; it is always idolatry.

   Idolatry always leads to pain and destruction, and as "The America Idol" is a specialty of the contemporary American Republican Party, we are well served to remember and remain guarded against this weakness. Every truth we seek and apply must first and always be done for the sake of honoring, obeying, and glorifying God. That is the only reason we should need (and must need) for doing, thinking, pursuing or even dreaming of anything.

2. **Our impulse to inappropriately mock or deride our opponents.** The pull of this temptation and the sinful results permeate the modern American political scene. While humor is a gift from God and certainly has a role to play in even serious discussions of weighty matters, there is no place for excessively crude mockery of people of any persuasion, as they are all image bearers (albeit broken ones) of the living God whom we serve and adore.

3. **Our expectation that our personal obedience to our Lord in any political matter is going to guarantee any particular result or "usher in the Kingdom" right here and now.** Our obedience to Christ in all things including the political is always to be pursued for the purpose of glorifying Him through our

obedience itself, and that is all the reason that we should ever need for our obedience. *Submission to Him is complete success.* What He chooses to do or not do with our beautiful act of obedient submission is His business, not ours, just as what He chooses to do or not do with our faithful proclamation of the Gospel is His business where the salvation of those who hear that Gospel proclamation is concerned. He commands. We obey. That is all. And it is more than enough...*infinitely* more...

We should not "settle" for this perspective; we should celebrate it, as its foundation of faith in the perfect plan and timing of our completely sovereign Lord is a matchless comfort and encouragement.

So what we're aiming for here, by God's grace, is something that is literally impossible without that grace: A Christ-centered perspective and confidence to share incredibly unpopular (and therefore long abandoned and mostly forgotten) truth, and the personal humility with which to maintain the primacy of Christ in everything from our larger long term goals to our daily demeanor.

Christ is our Lord, and that lordship is total. As such, His will must come to define our every thought, political or otherwise.

When's the last time you heard anything like *that* from a Republican seeking higher office?

When's the last time you even heard that sort of conversation unfold in the presence of such a Republican...without them squirming or shrieking like startled little girls while running for the safe, secular hills?

If there is any cooperative future of note to be had between biblical Christians in America and the contemporary American Republican Party, this has to change. God's expressed will and the pursuit of His glory must - as impossible as such a thing may seem at the moment - become the explicit, boldly, and openly proclaimed centerpiece of our political pursuits and policies.

Crazy talk?

Maybe...

...if you're a slave to the secular - secular standards, secular goals, secular pragmatism and all the rest...

But if you are a slave to Christ, it's the alternative that's crazy - you know, the alternative view that currently defines American culture.

This is why we're going to change the conversation in American politics. By God's grace and for His glory, we're going to proclaim His lordship and His Gospel at every opportunity. The world sees the pursuit of Christ in the politics as an improper imposition of God onto and into what man has worked oh so hard to set apart as his private, personal, self-serving little kingdom. As Christians, what we see in the political realm is another chance to proclaim His Gospel, advocate His truth, and glorify His nature through their explicit pursuit and proclamation at every opportunity.

After all, the pursuit of anything less on our part really would be crazy.

Or, to put a more appropriately positive spin on things, what would you like to look back on 100, 1,000, or 10,000 years from now - having passed on the opportunity to proclaim Christ's lordship in the political realm or having seized that opportunity to glorify His name and nature through your faithfulness in the face of great challenge and personal sacrifice?

The formal theological term for such a question is: "No brainer".

And with that perspective in hand, we are ready to consider those first goofy secular reactions that are bound to come our way when we actually engage the enemy, his ideas, and his pawns in the political realm.

CHRIST'S LORDSHIP: A POLITICAL HERESY

Let every person be subject to the governing authorities. **For there is no authority except from God, and those that exist have been instituted by God.** *Therefore whoever resists the authorities resists what God has appointed, and those who resist will incur judgment.* **For rulers are not a terror to good conduct, but to bad.** *Would you have no fear of the one who is in authority? Then do what is good, and you will receive his approval, for he is God's servant for your good. But if you do wrong, be afraid, for he does not bear the sword in vain.* **For he is the servant of God, an avenger who carries out God's wrath on the wrongdoer. Therefore one must be in subjection, not only to avoid God's wrath but also for the sake of conscience.**

ROMANS 13:1-5
(BOLD EMPHASIS ADDED)

It is much more grievous to offend the Creator than the creature, who is the image of the Creator.

JUNIUS BRUTUS, *A DEFENCE OF LIBERTY AGAINST TYRANTS*

Politics?!
No!
Religion?!
Well, maybe. We are supposed to be Christians, after all.
But politics *and* religion?!

Nooooooo ...and *no way...*and *what are you thinking by even proposing such a thing?*

It's religious heresy! It's politically incorrect! It's just...plain...wrong! Besides, if you actually speak of such things as these together, purposefully, everyone will hate you, everyone will mock you, and you just might even spontaneously combust from the sheer amount of entirely appropriate guilt you heap upon yourself in the process. So there!

That's the basic approach of the garden variety American "adult" these days when it comes to seeking out and considering deep truths. If the presentation of any particular subject can't be fit into a Super Bowl commercial or onto the back of a cereal box, we're just not interested. And if it can, it had better be funny or cute or sexyin its pitch. Without any of those three essential entertainment ingredients made available to escort a serious thought to our little brains, that thought has almost zero chance of even being allowed in the front door (as in, we just won't watch and we just won't listen). In other words, it had better be "relevant" to a people who just don't do serious anymore.

With generations of progressivism having taken its toll, advancing through the explicitly anti-Christian, state-controlled (and state-promoting) "education" system and the Hollywood/Madison Avenue entertainment and advertising industries, most Americans - including most American professing Christians, have freely and happily taken the progressive bait and have consequently bought into three rather profound lies regarding religion and politics:

1. **Religion and politics are each important, and as such are best handled by professionals.** Just as we are to trust seminary trained pros with our theology and our doctrine, and state chosen professionals with the education of our children, the protection of our borders, and the delivery of our mail.

2. **Religion and politics are each important, and as such should be sequestered or protected from interfering with one other.** The professionals have assured us that this is true, after all, and they *are* professionals.

3. **Religion and politics are each important, and as such are too deep for common people to properly understand, so common people shouldn't burden themselves with such considerations or related conversations.** Just leave it to the professionals. They'll take care of everything, so just run along and enjoy the game...or the movie...or the TV show...or *whatever*.

The professional political class in America is overrun with progressives. Both major parties, and most of the minor ones, too. The overwhelming majority of high traffic media. The even more overwhelming majority of those in the entertainment industry. All are squarely in the progressive camp.

Add to that roll call the accurate addition of most American professing Christian churches and their members, and you begin to see just how far gone we are; how late the hour really is. 100 years of progressivism and our near complete abdication of personal responsibility to the "pros" has left us teetering on the brink of oblivion on pretty much every level.

As a central part of their brilliant plan for liberating America from its cumbersome Christian heritage, progressive pros from all across the political and vocational spectrums have gone to great - and largely successful - lengths to get you and I and everyone else in their budding Ameritopia (thank you, Mark Levin) to just enjoy the bread and circuses and leave the important stuff to them. For just over a century, they've charted a decidedly progressive and explicitly anti-God course for the nation, and its people have played right along. Bread and circuses do have their charms, after all. And 100 years of progressive "education" has its benefits.

So it is that we've arrived at a time in America where talking about religion or politics is not a part of polite or even normal conversation, and talking about both together is unthinkable. And "unthinkable" tends to describe a large percentage of what used to be quite easily thinkable thoughts throughout American history - at least, before we progressed beyond the need for our masses to think.

At the end and by design, the typical American system drone is left with "unthinkable" responses to any number of questions and concepts that were once quite thinkable to even young children who were educated by their families according to Scripture in the age of American ascendancy. Where once we taught our own children *how* to think, we now trust The System and its pros to "teach" them *what* to think. Where once we were a nation of thinking individuals, we are now a managed gathering of regurgitating drones.

The socio-theological term for this is: Scary. *Really* scary. And the scariest part of this really scary situation is that we, as professing Christians in America, are far and away the single most responsible group of people for the nation's decline. We have not only allowed but encouraged and, in many cases, embraced, the lowly, shadowy, man-centered and God-mocking standards of progressivism.

As Christians, we are called to something higher; infinitely higher: The perfect standards of Jesus Christ and the true and perfect progress that they, and only they, can bring. We are called to proclaim His name and promote His glory in all things, taking "all thoughts captive", "tearing down enemy strongholds", and sharing His supernatural Gospel with a dying world in the process.

But a funny thing happened on the way to that Most High bar. More sad than funny, really, and more tragic than sad. Somewhere along the way, roughly a hundred years ago, Americans en masse decided that progress meant progress towards *themselves* - toward humanity, a path that always leads away from God. Where once even our most horrible errors and corrections were found out and fought over with Scripture as the ultimate guide, the era of progressivism was one of *man*-centered standards, *man*-centered goals, and *man*-centered dreams. It was, and is, all about *us*. In the worst deal since Manhattan went for a handful of beads, the faith of our founding was traded for a belief and system of man-centered, man-defined progress.

The progressive era stretches right into the very moment of this book's writing and is a prime reason for it having been written along with its sister work, *Satan's Jackass - The Progressive Party's War on Christianity*.

This is ***not*** a book aimed at convincing conservative Christians to vote for or against the Republican Party, for or against any other party, or to take and hold any specific position on any particular hot button political issue. Those things, worthy though they may be and appropriate as they are for other works, are ***not*** the point of *Stupid Elephant Tricks*.

The simple mission of this work is to inspire Christians - actual, Spirit-filled, supernaturally reborn New Creatures in Christ - to actively seek the will of their King in each and every thing - including each and every political thing - so that they might glorify Him and bless themselves and their culture through their obedience to His command to seek and submit to His perfect will in all things.

To that end, we will aim to encourage thought - explicitly Christ-centered thought - regarding a range of issues closely affiliated with contemporary American political conservatism. These issues are near and dear to the hearts of the progressive elitists currently dominating the leadership of the Republican Party, and they've done a fine job of convincing the rank and file that their progressive views are good, patriotic, and even Christian, in some sense or another.

As most Christians are rightly inclined in a very conservative political direction, their having been targeted for co-option by the right wing of the progressive movement should come as no surprise. The natural and proper conservatism of the biblical Christian has been used to great effect by the progressive pros to enlist their support in the advance of explicitly anti-Christian causes and standards.

That's what we're here to help correct, and we aim to do so by inspiring Christians to actively, boldly, clearly, and persistently seek the mind of Christ, share what they have learned and what they know with the world around them, and, in doing so, proclaim His truth and His Gospel through the innumerable opportunities that the world of politics provides for such supernaturally wonderful things.

Should a Christian base his political support for a party or cause or candidate on what God has revealed in His perfect Word?

Absolutely!

Should a Christian seek to better understand all political issues through the perfect light provided in God's perfect Word?

Ummm...hello? Is that a serious question?!

No, of course it's not. It's quite a silly one, actually, but it's the kind of silly question that is taken seriously today. And after it is taken seriously, it tends to be answered wrongly, even by most American professing Christians.

It all comes down to this: Do we believe that Jesus really is the perfect God; the Creator and Sustainer of all things, by whom and for whom they were all made for the express purpose of His self-glorification? Do we believe that He has commanded, for His glory and our benefit, that His truth and nature be pursued, proclaimed and exalted in all things, on all subjects, in all places and at all times? Do we seek to obey Him in this universal and universally important command?

Put another way: *Is He our Lord?*

Really?

To this we must answer, Oh yeah...*really!*

And we must demonstrate the reality of His lordship over us by obediently lifting His wisdom high in all places at all times, including the realm of American politics right now.

That's our goal in this little book and, Lord willing, it will be or become the goal of every reader who makes their way through these pages. We are not going to answer all, or even many, of the political questions posed here. What we are going to do here is ask some serious, important questions and then point toward the one and only completely reliable source for true answers to every critical question that can be asked: God's revealed will.

When a political party or cause seeks our support, we should first and always test them in light of His sufficient Word. When a candidate seeks our vote, we should first and always test them in light of His perfect Word. And when the opportunity comes to explore political issues in a conversation - *any* conversation - we should seek to guide all involved ever more toward the perfect light of Scripture, with the Gospel of Jesus Christ at the center of it all.

The nation is circling the drain and nearing its natural, dark end morally, economically, and spiritually. *What an opportunity!*

What an opportunity to proclaim His truth and explore His nature as they are presented in proper understandings of law, justice, love, family, marriage, sexuality, economics, liberty, freedom, and any other subject that swirls about in the heart of any political storm! We have every essential answer to every essential question, we have it perfectly in His Word, and we have the supernatural Gospel that can, by His grace, open the eyes of the lost so that they might see and love each and every one of those beautiful revelations.

All we need do is **submit** - submit in adoration of and confidence in our perfect King.

That loving submission is total victory...and it is impossible to have without seeking His will and proclaiming His glory in all things...including the world of American politics.

To that end and in these pages there are many very old questions to consider in a very new light. A perfect light. His perfect light.

Hope...change...revival...revolution... In seeking Him, we aim for the pure originals that have been so poorly counterfeited and successfully promoted throughout our sick and dying land for so very long. God-centered thought, God-centered hope, and God-centered change are our goals. God-centered revolution is fueled by such supernatural things as these.

We seek these things not first for love of country, or love of family, or hope for a prosperous future, but for the love of God Himself.

With Him as our one and only top and guiding priority, we are ready to roll. So let's get to it...

SECTION TWO

~

The Master and the Pretender

3

JESUS OWNS YOUR VOTE

A RE-INTRODUCTION TO THE OWNER OF THE POLITICAL REALM

"You shall love the Lord your God with all your heart and with all your soul and with all your mind. This is the great and first commandment."

JESUS (THE REAL ONE), IN MATTHEW 22:37-38

"It must be recognized that in any culture the source of law is the god of that society."

R.J. RUSHDOONY

Not since the first broadcast tales of unintended collisions between creamy milk chocolate and delicious peanut butter has there been a more oft repeated protestation regarding the improper mixture of one "good thing" with another. The televised pseudo-tragedies in question featured one person innocently enjoying their chocolate - usually a pretty sweet looking candy bar or something like that, while another obliviously slipped into an ecstasy coma by way of their favorite peanut butter. At this point in the stories, all seemed to be going so well in both creamy, delicious little worlds, and why wouldn't it? I mean, we're talking about chocolate and peanut butter here, right?

But just when both happy inhabitants of these two delicious dreamlands would hit high gear and begin to *really* enjoy their respective chocolaty/peanut buttery happy places...*whammo!* Things would get crazy. Really crazy.

We're talkin' world (and worldview) changing crazy.

While operating in a peanut butter or chocolate induced haze, one of these blissfully oblivious folks would run right into the other.

"You got your chocolate in my peanut butter!"

"You got your peanut butter in my chocolate!"

Thus climaxed the Reese's Peanut Butter Cups ads that were part of a scrumptiously successful candy selling campaign born in the '70s. As you might have guessed, the Reese's spin on this collision of previously comfortably independent worlds was one that ultimately celebrated the unexpected, supercool consequences of this game changing, world mixing event. The two delicious lands, despite the protestations of each of their happy, protective inhabitants, came together in the end to form a new thing that was much better than the old. And that incredible thing, in this case the peanut butter cup, went on to sell very, very well and make many people very, very happy, thank you very much. TV dramatizations can move people that way, as we all know.

While the beautiful mix of PB and C that is the Reese's Cup has gone on to much success and glory, a far more serious matter regarding the quarantine of one world from another has been the focus of not one, but many media campaigns. These campaigns go on today en masse. And the perspective that they advocate has taken deep root in both of the worlds targeted for influence.

"You keep your religion out of my politics!"

"You keep your politics out of my religion!"

Democrats say these things. Republicans say these things. Professing Christians say these things. Actual Christians say these things. Pretty much everyone in America seems to say these things. They say them, in most cases, out of habit, tradition, and reflex. They say them as a part of a deeply held, but often not very deeply thought out, desire to "protect" one world from the influence of the other.

From the typical secular perspective, whatever Christians do in the portions of their lives that seem to unfortunately intersect with politics, they should be discouraged, if not prohibited, from allowing them to make a public impact. Their Jesus and His extremist religious views cannot be allowed to be too awful much of an influence on the culture, and "too awful much of an influence" tends to translate into pretty much any public action or expressed opinion that contradicts or conflicts with the secular sensibilities that have come to captivate and define the contemporary American political scene. You can have your religion if you must, Christians, just be sure to keep it out of your *actual political views in practice* regarding things like...

- **Infanticide**

- **Marriage**

- **Family**

- **Education**

- **Economics**

- **Homosexuality**

- **Welfare State Slavery**

- **Freedom of Speech** (Which includes that pesky "freedom to publically proclaim the unpopular Gospel" thing.)

So, you see, Christians, you can have your Christianity, so long as you keep it from actually, *in practice*, touching any important area of public or cultural life. Oh sure, you can talk about these

THE MASTER AND THE PRETENDER

subjects in your churches and homes if you must - for now. But whatever you do, don't dare go falling for the suspicious (and most *non-progressive*) notion that you should actually run around the countryside freely and happily aiming to influence the political thoughts of others as a part of that super-wacky, crazy-extremist "Jesus is Lord over *all*" thing. Just stay in your churches, sit in your pews, sing your silly little songs on Sundays, and leave all of the important stuff to us. And by "us" we mean, practically, the masses minus you. Everybody wins this way. You get your churches and homes (for now), and we get the world. Now *that's* progressive!

Be practical. Be pragmatic. Be reasonable and realistic. And be all of these things as they are *secularly* defined, which is another way of saying, "Be progressive".

TRICKS, TREATS, AND TRADES

"Because our Lord is God, and there is none other, every word of Scripture is a binding word, a command word, that requires us to hear and obey. We dare not reduce the faith to pious gush, nor worship to an aesthetic experience. The purpose of the church's services is not an impressive musical or liturgical treat but to provide marching orders to the soldiers of Christ."

R.J. RUSHDOONY

One guiding battle-cry and banner of the Christian life that we'll be aiming to exalt and hold high throughout this book is the fact that Jesus truly is, in reality, Lord over *all*. He rules and reigns over *every* realm and *every* area of life, and this is a truth that

Christian's should aim to live out and love in every moment of every day. Even when they're voting...or talking politics...or thinking politics...or...well, you get the picture.

There is no part or portion or partitioned off little piece of our lives as individuals or as a culture that we can sequester from His explicit rule and authority and expect anything better than a catastrophic result. As Christians, we understand and are to proclaim and live out the truth that submission to Him as Lord over *all* is the only path to true peace, joy, happiness and fulfillment in any arena or aspect of life. This God-centered perspective is the heart of biblical Christianity. This God-centered perspective is also the first and most persistent target of all things "progressive".

The more we come to understand the true nature of progressive tolerance and the true nature of progressive political goals, the more clearly we will begin to see many things - many very important things that have been ignored or dismissed by many American Christians for a very long time. We have ignored these realities to the great detriment of the nation and culture in which we live - the nation and culture which we are called to transform in His name and for His glory. By God's grace, the fog will begin to lift as we explore a variety of issues here, and as that fog is swept away for those who know and love Him as Lord, we will begin to see the need and opportunity for action - action aimed at, above all else, obedience to Him and, Lord willing, action that can and will make a supernaturally positive impact on the otherwise doomed nation that is "progressive America".

We've been sold a bundle of lies, and, as the twelve-steppers like to say, our first step towards a solution will be to recognize that we have a problem. As Christians, it is critical that this recognition be followed by repentance.

We must recognize and repent of having ever believed the notion that we should abstain from explicitly seeking and exalting His perfect will in all things. This is vital, and the beautiful relationship that He has given us finds ongoing and ever growing strength throughout our constant (meaning daily, at the very least) repentance and seeking after conformity to His will. We all fail at achieving this perfect conformity daily, and we all grow in that conformity daily if we repent of our failures daily. This is one great beauty of what we know as true progress - that is, progress toward Christ-likeness. This is the progress that we must seek in all places, at all times, and in all parts of the lives that He has made and given to us.

We must repent of having ever thought that we could vote for a man to lead the nation without considering above all else the question, "Who does he say that Jesus is?"

We must repent of having ever allowed for weak, watery professions of a largely undefined faith in an even less explicitly defined Jesus to pass for the bold, clear, God-glorifying testimony that should be essential for us to support anyone who would seek to hold high office in our land.

We must repent of having ever questioned the notion that Christ is the *essential* core of knowledge, wisdom, and education in *all* things.

We must repent of having ever placed our material wealth above - *far above* - our explicit glorification of God as individuals and as a people.

We must repent of having ever allowed the state to grow into the explicitly anti-Christian beast that it has become. And we must constantly seek to reform and conform our understanding and pursuit in all areas so that we might not only, by His grace, reverse the impossibly dark situation in which we find ourselves, but never again chart this path to Christ-less "progress".

We've been deceived because, in self-righteous pride, we've signed up for deception. We've traded the truth of His lordship for the lie of our own. In this, we, as professing American Christians, have sinned against a holy God and are even now watching our hard earned and catastrophically consequential chickens come home to roost.

But this is hardly the end of the story. At least it need not be for those of us who are in Him and placed here in this time and in this place for His specific purposes. For us, the other side of repentance and humbly seeking His will holds matchless joy, power, and potential - the potential to seek and do His will for His glory rather than our own.

This is our (and our nation's) Mission: Impossible made possible in Him.

AMERICAN REPENTANCE, REFORMATION, AND REVIVAL

"I tremble for my country when I reflect that God is just, that His justice cannot sleep forever."

THOMAS JEFFERSON

"America will never be destroyed from the outside. If we falter and lose our freedoms, it will be because we destroyed ourselves."

ABRAHAM LINCOLN

"Whatever we once were, we are no longer a Christian nation."

BARACK OBAMA

All of our sins regarding government and national policies are symptomatic of a larger lie having taken root. They are sinful side-effects of one great and evil-enabling principle that the vast majority of Americans - both secular and Christian - have bought into hook, line, and stinking sinker. It is the great, delusional deception at the heart of every Stupid Elephant Trick. It is the satanic notion that Christ need not be embraced as Lord over *all*.

You may have detected the lordship of Christ over *all* as a theme here. If so, you have discerned wisely. The lordship of Christ in the political realm is the drumbeat we aim to encourage here. It is in this Spirit that we will aim to grind the notion that "Christianity is a private matter" deep under our heels as we march along.

In our silence, we have denied Him, and in our denial of His lordship, we have sought to make ourselves lords - pathetic, silent, sad little go-along-to-get-along lords over "our parts" of His creation. In claiming such power over a part - or even the *ability* to claim it - we have, in reality, claimed the whole. We have made ourselves god.

This is the mad delusion that has fueled all anti-Christian "progress" throughout the ages, from the fall of Lucifer right on through to today. The idea that any creation can rightly rule in a manner contrary to Christ in any way in any part of His creation is the foundation upon which all Christ-less "progress" is built. This is the heart of rebellion and the core of sin: That any creation should be exalted as the standard setting definer of truth. We must face the fact that we, as professing Christians in America, have done a most terrible thing by denying Him as Lord over *all*. We must face this fact...and we must repent.

Then, and only then, on the other side of our brokenness and His grace through our restoration, things are gonna get *really* good...

SUPERNATURAL REVOLUTIONARIES

"We are not diplomats but prophets, and our message is not a compromise but an ultimatum."

A.W. Tozer

"God is most glorified in us when we are most satisfied in Him"

John Piper

So we're living in a nation teetering on the brink of economic collapse, already plunged through the moral, ethical floor and on into a dungeon of a senselessness and sensuality drenched reality. Postmodern relativism has disassembled every truth and, in doing so, has disconnected our culture from truth and its Author.

True beauty...gone.

True art...gone.

True peace...gone.

True freedom...gone.

True joy...gone.

In seeking to define beauty, art, peace, freedom, and joy on *our* terms and clinging to those self-set standards as our guiding principles, we have lost sight of every true original and been left holding and living, for a while, by the fading light of pathetic counterfeits. And once the fade finishes, as it is at this very moment across the American culture, then final darkness will, and should, fall upon us.

As fallen people, we know that we are doomed. The situation is impossibly dark and desperate. There is no hope.

As supernaturally reborn New Creatures in Christ, we know that He has this world right where He wants it! He has us right where He wants us and His perfect plan for the ultimate restoration of all things and His perfect glorification is right...on...schedule.

Put another way, we have everything to hope, cheer, and thank Him for right now, *especially* since He has seen fit to put us here in this time and in this place for His perfect purposes.

So perfect is the weaponry that He has equipped us with for the battles to come that we only need one: His perfect Word, which contains His perfect Gospel.

This is the weapon we will bring to bear in every conflict. This is the perfect standard against which we will test *all* things...every candidate....every policy...every plan....*everything*.

With His supernatural Gospel, we will raise dead men to life and, Lord willing, a dead nation into a God-glorifying one. With His Word we will seek His will in all matters of our governance wherever He has given us the power to do so.

With His perfect Word as our guide, we will endeavor to elect Christ-centered leaders to chart a Christ-centered path to true progress, all for the glory of God and to the benefit of our people.

With His perfect Word as our light, we will chart an economic path that leads both individuals and our nation from the twin slaveries of debt and the Welfare State. We will chart an explicitly Christ-centered path of education and growth for our children, living out the truth that "The fear of the Lord is the beginning of knowledge" and "the beginning of wisdom". And we will successfully defend the right of innocent image-bearers of God to the life He has given them while preserving the God-ordained families in which they will be nurtured in the knowledge and love of His truth.

Contrary to popular - and stupid elephant - opinion, these victories are possible. But only by His grace, according to His will, and through His supernatural Gospel. By His grace, we are in a land where, for the moment, His Gospel can be legally and publically proclaimed. But this is changing - the sands are shifting against us, and quickly...

JESUS OWNS YOUR VOTE

Time is short.

The enemy's grip is tightening.

The race is on.

The time is *now!*

We have the power, the opportunity, and the *responsibility* to seize this moment, not first for ourselves, or for America, or even for our families, but for our God. That is the spirit that must motivate this mission if it is to be successful.

Remember: America has no Caesar...but she can, and soon. We the people have been graced by our God with a blessing unknown to the great majority of humanity throughout its history - the power to shape and participate in our own national government. Insofar as we use this gift to glorify Him, we will be blessed. Insofar as we neglect the responsibilities that come with this power He has graciously given us, we will lose it. And insofar as we use this power to promote Christ-less anything, we will bring His judgment upon ourselves and our children.

We have a mission, and that mission is both simple and profound: To glorify God and exalt the name of Christ in all places and at all times.

Encouraging and equipping the Believer for this great and beautiful task as it relates to the current political scene in America is the aim of *Stupid Elephant Tricks - The Other Progressive Party's War on Christianity*, as well as its sister work, *Satan's Jackass - The Progressive Party's War on Christianity*. Each of these books focuses on the unique, yet overlapping characteristics of the progressive movement as embodied by the two major, and ruling, political parties in America at the time of this writing. While neither work is aimed at the deep exploration of political theory or Christian theology, it is hoped that they will help to spark in the reader a passion for the will of God to be known and pursued, happily and adoringly, in all times, and places and *politics*, and all for His glory.

To that end, the reader is reminded that this book is written by a profoundly flawed man. So do be diligent to seek Scripture on every subject covered and test everything written here in the perfect light of that perfect Word.

With that essential reminder in place, we are off to do some dragon slaying...one exposed trick at a time...beginning with a favorite of the good ol' boys' Grand Old Party: The myth of a helpful, but Christ-less conservatism...

THE STUPID ELEPHANT IN THE ROOM

AN INTRODUCTION TO CHRIST-LESS CONSERVATISM

"Conservatism is the solution for the world's problems."

RUSH LIMBAUGH

"…it's not about our faith, it's about our principles. I just want to know that a man believes in something…and will actually stand up for what he believes in. That's the way you vote for President."

GLENN BECK

*And whatever you do, in word or deed, **do everything in the name of the Lord Jesus**, giving thanks to God the Father through him.*

COLOSSIANS 3:17 (BOLD EMPHASIS ADDED)

America is a Christian nation. And I am Napoleon Bonaparte. Or maybe you're Napoleon Bonaparte. Or maybe we're both Easter

Bunnies. Or Jedi knights from a long time ago in a galaxy far, far away. Whatever the case, while each of these suggestions may seem a bit ludicrous, only one is flat out nuts.

If you need a hint as to which one pegs the "flat out nuts" meter, just head to a mall. A nice mall. A high end, "high quality" mall in a typical high end, high quality American community. Just wander on over there and have a look-see...at least as much as you can before the Spirit convicts you of...well...any number of things. Like what people are wearing. Or how people are acting. Or what businesses are selling. Or how those businesses are advertising what they're selling.

Even as you read the last sentence or two, it was likely that you were bracing for the bit to follow, not necessarily for fear of the shock, but for fear of...boredom. Such is the state of our desensitization to what passes for clothing, style, and advertising today in "Christian America". The sensuality-soaked stylings of American pop-culture have become so common for so long that most of us hardly flinch anymore when we see or hear about them. Many of the most popular branded fashions of today, if they were worn by anyone publically in America just 50 or 60 years ago, their chosen "style" would have inspired either their arrest for indecency or their institutionalization for suspected insanity. Really.

Yet at our fine American shopping malls, we have, for every stroller-riding toddler to see...Victoria's Secret. Yessiree, we proudly (and profitably) plant scores of nearly nude models posed seductively all around the primo spots in our most prized public shopping areas here in "Christian America".

And the Victoria's Secret approach to advertising is hardly limited to Victoria's Secret product types. It is now used to sell everything from candy and shoes to soap and cheeseburgers. When it comes to expressions of disdain for the crystal clear pronouncements on modesty, sensuality, sexuality and decency from the God of biblical Christianity, we couldn't be more clear if we tried. "Christian America" takes every opportunity to openly mock and defy the God of *actual* Christianity.

Truth be told - and that is the goal here - this naked display of prostitution-esque skin-for-cash is a demonstration of fidelity to America's *actual* god, since, as any honest observer would be quick to notice and confirm, America's god is money. Material prosperity. Things. Stuff. Much more on this later, but one point worthy of consideration early in our journey is that of America's "Christian Nation" identity as contrasted with those nations who openly claim Islam as their religion and Allah as their god.

Without doing a deep survey or study at the moment, we are well served to consider the following related questions: Which nation, if any, is serious about their religion? Which nation actually trusts in and believes upon its god? Which nation takes its "holy texts" seriously?

Which nation could then be said to actually love its god?

Of all the things one might say about many of the stereotypical radical Islamist descriptions of America, when it comes to the oft-repeated contention that America is a purveyor of vice and ungodliness without peer, we might call the Islamist "angry", "extreme" or maybe even "hateful", but one thing we cannot credibly label them as in such an instance is "wrong". America simply *is* a sin-drenched, sin-loving, and sin-promoting society. That much seems undeniably true.

Whatever one thinks of Islam, Allah, the Koran, or any other Islamic thing, what must be acknowledged is that Muslim nations tend to take all of those things seriously. Very seriously. As for America and her relationship with Christianity, its Bible and its God, well...

One need hardly possess a professorial grasp of Christian history or America's present in order to realize that the modern U. S. of A. is about as consecrated to Christ as the modern Madonna is committed to chastity. It is at this point of realization that we should proceed with caution, however, lest we be tempted to chase any number of interesting, yet distracting, little rabbits 'round the track of political or philosophical or sociological contemplation.

We might righteously (and rightly) complain about the decline of American culture, the death of American morality, and the collapse of the American work ethic while simultaneously parading and bemoaning an impressive list of examples to support our good and proper whining. Yep, that would certainly be doable, and it has been done...again and again.

We might also go the rant and rail route against the contemporary American obsession with increasingly dark and destructive entertainment, and the Hollywood/Madison Avenue monstrosity that specializes in fueling the pop-culture bullet-train to hell. Yeah, we could go there. And most of us have...again and again.

We might even get a bit more specific and focus on what we see as the clear and explicitly anti-Christian agenda of the contemporary American Left, as championed by the modern Progressive movement and aggressively implemented by the American Democrat political party. We'd certainly not be lacking for a long list of clear, stirring, and even stunning examples to support our complaint-o-rama on that front as well.

We could talk about the impending economic collapse of the nation. We could go on and on about the carefully crafted slave state of dependants that makes that collapse inevitable. We could talk about the disintegration of the family and the subsequent destruction of the very foundations of society. In each of these areas we could easily lay the blame for every catastrophic consequence under consideration squarely at the feet of "The Left" or "The Progressives" or [insert preferred bad guy group here]. And in each of these areas we could promote our own, often good and Bible-based, solutions; our favored ways of saving the economy, restoring the family, and reclaiming the culture.

We could present to this tailspinning world the beauty of Bible-based wisdom as it has been graciously revealed to us regarding everything from family and fidelity to economy and philosophy, hoping and praying that our good, God-inspired advice will be taken in time to avoid the looming collapse that we all sense is imminent. We could bring light to these subjects and literally avert the disaster to come...if only the world would listen.

See that?

See the danger? Feel the pull? The urge to chase the decoy?

See how interesting those little rabbits and their trails of distraction can be? They're nearly irresistible to us, yet resist them we must. We have to be diligent. We have to stay frosty and keep our eye on the prize; the prize being the one and only true solution with the supernatural power to save our nation and culture, one individual at a time. The prize that is the Gospel of Jesus Christ.

IT'S *NOT* THE ECONOMY, STUPID

So Jesus said to the Jews who had believed him, "If you abide in my word, you are truly my disciples, and you will know the truth, and the truth will set you free."

JOHN 8:31-32

Amazing grace! How sweet the sound
That saved a wretch like me!
I once was lost, but now am found,
Was blind, but now I see.

AMAZING GRACE, BY JOHN NEWTON

"If only the world would listen."

There is the problem. And there is the fork in the road.

To the left, there is the wide road - a pathway open to the discussion and pursuit of every solution impacting nearly every single subject of significance. Every weighty area is covered; at least all but one. Sociology, philosophy, economics, ethics...they're all addressed, and in perfect, vivid detail. We've got the books, the seminars, the sermons, and the DVD sets to prove it. We have all that we could possibly need to make solid, biblical arguments for solid, biblical pursuits in every realm of life, which is another way of saying that we have the perfect blueprint and plan for the actual realization of truly and perfectly happy, joyous, fulfilling lives. We really do. That's just how good our God has been to us.

With this in mind, it's easy to understand our enthusiasm for sharing these matchlessly empowering and joyful concepts. What better or more desperately needed gift could there be than that of a *guaranteed* remedy for the faltering American family? Or the collapsing American culture? Or the imploding American economy?

Glad you asked. The answer to that seemingly rhetorical question is critical to our identifying and understanding the primary problem and its only solution...a problem and solution that every rabbit and rabbit trail aims to obscure and conceal.

There are many problems - *serious* problems - facing the nation and the world, to be sure. But there is one great malady - The Problem - above all others, and it stands as the impenetrable barrier between all other problems and their true and lasting solutions.

The collapse of the family is not The Problem. The abandonment of virtue is not The Problem. The collapse of the economy is not The Problem.

The Problem is sin. And our culture is filled with people who are literally enslaved to sin and spiritually dead. They may be walking and talking and buying and watching and reading (?) and smiling and joking and the like, but, make no mistake, they are *dead*. This is the most tragic of realities with which we must contend. This is the saddest of realities that literally defines the nature and existence of unconverted Americans - many professing Christianity - who comprise the vast majority of the nation's population. Biblically, we must recognize that The Problem with

America is that it is filled with and dominated by spiritually dead people.

This is both a great tragedy and a great opportunity...if we will simply open our eyes, obey our King, and embrace the mission He has so perfectly set before us.

Somewhere along the way, we've been profoundly distracted from the reality that the "truth that sets us free" cannot be seen, much less understood, until there is a supernatural act of God upon the life of the spiritually dead creature in question; a supernaturally imposed rebirth that gives the formerly dead man or woman eyes to see, ears to hear, and a heart to desire truth and its Author for the first time. Somewhere along the way, we lost sight of the fact that the only way we have - the only message we've been given - that is guaranteed by God to raise the spiritually dead to life and give them those eyes, ears, and hearts, is the whole, undiluted Gospel of Jesus Christ.

RAISING THE DEAD - GOD'S SPECIALITY

The hearing ear and the seeing eye,
the LORD has made them both.

Proverbs 20:12

For this people's heart has grown dull, and with their
ears they can barely hear, and their eyes they have
closed,
lest they should see with their eyes and hear with their
ears
and understand with their heart and turn, and I would
heal them.' But blessed are your eyes, for they see, and
your ears, for they hear.

Matthew 13:15-16

We begin to see the source of our problem - the inspiration of our distractions - when we take a closer, prayerful look at the objects of our affection in so many of our cultural or political pursuits. The family, the economy, the culture in general...all of these are certainly areas of great importance and very much worthy of our attentiveness. The problem that we face is not the serious consideration or treatment of serious subjects, it is the exaltation of those areas above the one object of affection that must always remain in the premier position, namely, Christ.

The nature of Christ and His perfect Gospel is the prism through which all else is rightly considered, and, contrary to the impulses or opinions of some, "all else" includes the family, the economy, the culture, and any other sub-realm included in and impacted by the sphere known as the world of politics.

When we understand and embrace core components of the perfect, supernatural Gospel, we see the world rightly. When we use the perfect light He has provided in His Word, we are never led astray. And when we see that, according to His perfect revelation, all men are born spiritually dead, hating holiness and loving sin by nature, that in this condition they are literally blind to the beauty and truth of the Kingdom of God, and that the only solution to this walking-dead condition is the supernatural Gospel of Jesus Christ, then we should have little trouble realizing that before any walking-dead, God-hating, sin-loving creature could possibly play any sort of truly lasting, impactful role in the restoration of the culture at large, they must first individually be supernaturally resurrected from spiritual death to life by God through the means by which He has ordained such supernatural transformations to occur: The presentation of the Gospel.

The whole, undiluted Gospel. The *exclusive* Gospel. The *divisive* Gospel. The *brutal and beautiful* Gospel. The *supernatural* Gospel.

As Christians, this is our first essential tool; our only hope of victory in the reclamation of all realms for the Kingdom of Christ, including the political.

Dead men need a supernatural solution before they can actually live, and they must be alive in the true, biblical, spiritual sense, before they can be counted upon for anything truly good and lasting. This is the truth that those pesky rabbits aim to obscure at all costs, and this is the truth that we must embrace if we are to, above all else, obey and honor our Lord. If through that obedience He chooses to restore a multitude of American families, resurrect the American culture, or revive the dying American economy, then so be it. Praise God! But however much we may rightly and reasonably desire these results, they are *not* to be our measure of success.

Obedience to God *is* success.

100%.

And we must *never* lose sight of this...lest those rabbits have their way with us...again.

RABBIT TRAILS AND ELEPHANT TRICKS

He who has ears to hear, let him hear!

MATTHEW 11:15

Now when Jesus came into the district of Caesarea Philippi, he asked his disciples, "Who do people say that the Son of Man is?" 14 And they said, "Some say John the Baptist, others say Elijah, and others Jeremiah or one of the prophets." 15 He said to them, "But who do you say that I am?" 16 Simon Peter replied, "You are the Christ, the Son of the living God." 17 And Jesus answered him, "Blessed are you, Simon Bar-Jonah! For flesh and blood has not revealed this to you, but my Father who is in heaven.

MATTHEW 16:13-17

*For by him all things were created, in heaven and on earth, visible and invisible, whether thrones or dominions or rulers or authorities—all things were created through him and **for him**.*

COLOSSIANS 1:16

The more we come to understand and embrace the revelation that *all* pure truth and beauty is completely rooted in Christ, and that He has both charged us with a supernatural mission and equipped us with a supernatural tool (His Gospel), the more we will come to realize that we are *perfectly* equipped to conquer every realm that He would call us to enter...including the political realm.

Before going on further, we should note that the political realm is simply another way of describing the process or philosophy of the government of a people. The realm of politics directly aims to impact our lives on every front - our families, our work, our economics, our plans, our dreams, our goals, our freedom of expression, our physical health...our *everything*. Even the dominion of our thought life is sought by political activists. The political realm overlaps parts of every other, thus our political perspectives impact all other perspectives.

So it is that the Bible is a very political book, and Christianity is a very political way of life.

While such a statement may inspire something of a gag reflex from many a good Brother or Sister in Christ, the importance of Christians actively seeking to do the will of their Lord with all their mind, all their spirit, all their body, and all their strength at all times is undeniable. With this crucial concept completely embraced, we understand that it is simply impossible to fully honor Christ without explicitly honoring Him in every thought and deed, which includes, of course, every *political* thought and every *political* deed. More specifically for the American Christian, this includes how they vote, as their vote belongs to their King, Jesus the Christ.

Put another way, we are to love the Lord with all our heart, mind, body, and *vote*. The political power that we have been given is a gift from Him, and we are each individually responsible to Him for our good use of that gift.

As American Christians, we have been uniquely, providentially, and intentionally positioned in this place, at this time, and with this power for a purpose. *His* purpose. Every cultural crisis is an opportunity first and foremost for His people to proclaim His Gospel and celebrate His nature. As American Christians, we have been blessed in a manner unknown to the vast majority of people who have come and gone throughout history.

We who know Him as "the way, the truth, and the life" should understand - more so with every day spent walking with Him and studying His Word - that without Him on the throne of one's own life, every pursuit is ultimately futile.

Every economic pursuit, every moralistic pursuit, every artistic pursuit, every literary pursuit, every academic pursuit...all of it is for nothing without Him as its acknowledged source and ultimate goal. This is a reality that must inform the Christian political ethic, and it is a reality that, when embraced, will prevent us from falling for any number of tricks, be they rabbit or elephant related.

All of the rabbit trails planted to divert our attention from the one true path to which we are called share one common attribute: They are creation-focused rather than Creator-focused.

Our desires for a restored economy are reasonable, wise, and good insofar as they actively and explicitly exalt Christ first and throughout their pursuit. Our hopes for restored, vibrant marriages and families are wonderful and right, insofar as they actively and explicitly pursue Christ first and always. Our dreams of a revived American culture are ever so sound and sweet, so long as they actively and explicitly center on Christ and His glory from beginning to end.

It is when we shift away from explicitly Christ-centered perspectives in these areas that our pursuits, however right and good they may sound or seem to the undiscerning mind, are, in reality, seeds of destruction.

Any economic solution that does not explicitly exalt and seek the will of Christ is, in fact, evil and doomed to ultimate failure. The same is true of all other pursuits of restoration, revival, or reformation. The claim that any truly good thing can be seen, much less understood or pursued, apart from the nature of Christ and submission to His will, is a lie first conceived and successfully marketed by the father of lies. This lie, first spoken by the serpent in the garden, echoes throughout America and the world today. As we will cover in some detail, this fundamental deceit is foundational to the political philosophy of the contemporary American Republican Party, and until we recognize this profound problem and seek its correction through repentance and the subsequent unobstructed and unambiguous pursuit of Christ in all things, we will continue to fall for any number of distractions and diversions offered by every enemy of Christ and the advance of His Kingdom.

In *Stupid Elephant Tricks*, we will be examining the unique problem posed by the contemporary American Republican Party and its approach to...well...pretty much *everything*. The underlying reason for the pervasiveness of "The Republican Problem" is directly attached to the point we've focused on up to now, namely, the preeminence of Christ as Lord and the explicit embrace of His perfect, supernatural Gospel as the essential, exclusive cure for the root cause of all political problems and cultural afflictions, also known as "sin". The Republican aversion to these essential truths while pretending to offer valid solutions or paths to victory over any particular problem facing the nation and its people is patently absurd. More importantly, it is dangerous. Most importantly, it is an offense to Christ. And therefore, it should be an offense to His people.

In a related, if not identical, spirit to that which motivates the contemporary American Democrat Party, the Republican Establishment has charted an explicitly progressive path for America - all while simultaneously paying lip service to "God" (however you choose to define Him) and avoiding explicit service to the Lord Jesus Christ. Just as the American political Left opts for explicitly Christ-less "progress", so does its political Right. The primary party of the Left, the Democrat Party, is the focus of a simultaneously released book, *Satan's Jackass - The Progressive Party's War on Christianity*. The prime political party of the American Right, the Republican Party, is the focus of this work, and while, according to popular opinion, the two parties in question occupy diametrically opposed positions on most important issues and concepts, we will endeavor to uncover and explore here the reality that they are, in truth, two wings of the same Christ-less creature. As such, they share several key attributes that will be covered here in some detail, including:

1. **A commitment to Christ-less thought and conversation.** All serious dialogue pursued by both parties is deliberately and purposefully sterilized of any specifically Christ-centered content. Vague appeals to a god or God or singing of "God Bless America" are substituted for - but not to be confused with - the essential, explicit exaltation of Jesus Christ as Lord over all. The purposeful avoidance of the exaltation of the exclusive Christ of Scripture is hardly a problem that is unique to the Democrat Party. It's one of the elephant's favorite stupid tricks.

2. **A commitment to creation worship rather than Creator worship.** Where the new-agey Left tends to fix its affection and attention on the physical creation of God (as in "Mommy Earth" worship or "save the whales" obsessions), the Christ-less Right loudly and proudly worships non-material creations such as the concepts of individual liberty and free markets. As we will see, it is no less a sin to worship or exalt a non-material creation above the Creator than it is to exalt or worship a material creation above the Creator. To claim that America can find anything resembling the "freedom" or "liberty" so often advertised by the Republican Party apart from the explicit exaltation of Christ in such a pursuit is an approach that epitomizes the Satanic worldview.

3. **A commitment to Christ-less "solutions".** By way of secularly defined pragmatism, itself defining every bit of dialogue and approach regarding every solution to every problem, the contemporary American Republican Party has charted a path to an explicitly Christ-less destination. The route may be quite different from that preferred by the party of the Left, but the destination is the same.

Each of these areas will be addressed in the pure light of biblical truth, and each of these three areas will be addressed in light of corresponding correctives taken from Scripture, including:

1. **The nature of Christ.** The Lord Jesus Christ will be explicitly exalted and sought after as the source and object of all good and right things, including all of those included in the political realm (a realm no less His than any other).

2. **The power of His Gospel.** The supernatural Gospel will be explored and presented as the first essential cure to the problem at the root of all problems, political or otherwise, namely: sin.

3. **The responsibility of His people.** The unique opportunity that we have been given as American Christians is one precious reality for which we will praise Him throughout the eternity to come. We are here in this desperate situation in this darkened land for the greatest of purposes: The exaltation of Christ. We can and must seize every opportunity to glorify Him, and that truth must guide our political thoughts and actions just as it does any other. By His grace and for His glory, we have been given this opportunity and this responsibility.

While on the topic of opportunity, let us take a moment to celebrate the place in which we find ourselves. Far from despairing at the sight of a culture in ruin or an economy on the edge of oblivion or a nation seemingly dominated by and dedicated to the pursuit of Christ-less "progress", we, as those whom He has purposefully placed at this time and in this place with these political powers and opportunities, should embrace them all for His name and glory.

As we enter into that sweetest and most encouraging of embraces, we will find ourselves less and less impressed with or distracted by the Christ-less promises and diversions of any counter-Christian group or individual. We will simply stride past the attempts to divert and go about the business of "bringing down enemy strongholds" and "taking every thought captive" for Christ, and we will do so through the proclamation of the one and only true solution to every sin-fueled problem that has come to define and dominate our nation and culture. We embrace and deploy the perfect, supernaturally powerful weapon with which we have been equipped: The whole, undiluted Gospel of Jesus Christ.

GOSPEL BEAUTY, POWER, AND LIBERATION

so shall my word be that goes out from my mouth;
  it shall not return to me empty,
but it shall accomplish that which I purpose,
  and shall succeed in the thing for which I sent it.

ISAIAH 55:11

For the word of God is living and active, sharper than any two-edged sword, piercing to the division of soul and of spirit, of joints and of marrow, and discerning the thoughts and intentions of the heart.

HEBREWS 4:12

Hand in glove with the biblical repudiation and dismissal of every proposed Christ-less "solution" offered by the Republican (or any other) Party must come an ever-increasing understanding and admiration of the whole, true Gospel. While we will explore this fundamental truth in detail later, there is one important aspect of the Gospel that we should explore here at the outset.

While we are commanded to proclaim the beautiful, supernatural Gospel of Christ to the world, we are *not* to use the world's standards of measurement where our ideas of "success" are concerned. Put another way, our obligation and mission is to proclaim the truth; the results are all up to God. This is both an ultimately liberating and encouraging reality when it is rightly understood.

The bottom line - and one that will be reiterated and expressed throughout this book - is that, as a Christian man, woman, boy, or girl, our one and only standard and measure of success is personal obedience. When we obey Him faithfully and completely, we have attained perfect and total success. We have hit the center of the bull's-eye. We have scored the perfect grade. We have won. Completely. By His grace and for His glory.

This seems such a simple thing, yet it stands in stark contrast to the modern American mindset, which is drenched in and defined by secular pragmatism, a subject that will also be explored in some detail later. This Americanized pragmatism is almost always inclined, and strongly so, towards the measurement of success in terms of numbers; usually in tallies of people (church attendance, "conversions", professions of faith, etc.) or dollars ("tithes" and offerings, building funds funded, etc.). This secular standard must be consciously discarded and trampled underfoot by the Christian, lest they find themselves burdened by utterly unbiblical pressures and wooed by any of the many explicitly anti-Christian spins on the Gospel that have come to define much of contemporary American Christianity.

The consequences of dismissing or halfheartedly embracing this core truth can be catastrophic. If we believe that we are the one who must accomplish any result of the Gospel, then we are bound to do as most contemporary American churches have done by altering, tweaking and basically abandoning the undiluted - and incredibly offensive to a fallen world - Gospel of Jesus Christ.

When we realize that the results of our obedience in proclaiming His Gospel are assured, *not* by us (or our articulation or our intelligence or our charisma), but by *Him*, and by Him *entirely*, then we are much more likely to, by His grace, boldly take the brutal truth of His Gospel to a world that, quite frankly, hates it and will hate us for sharing it with them...until and unless He chooses to supernaturally save those who hear it through our faithful proclamation.

With the true Gospel as the first essential component in the cure for sinfulness - the affliction at the root of every cultural problem engulfing our nation and the world - we will then be able to effectively and coherently point further towards the nature of Christ in His perfect revelation (the Word) as we tackle many of the pressing political issues of our day, including:

- **The Sanctity of Life**
- **The Sanctity of Marriage**
- **The State of the Family**
- **The Economy**
- **The Slave/Welfare State**
- **The Nanny/Big Brother State**

Each and every one of these areas of concern offers, above all else, an incredible opportunity for the proclamation of the Gospel and the exaltation of the nature of Christ in the pursuit of their solutions. Insofar as we who call Him Lord seize this moment and these opportunities to proclaim His Gospel and truth to a dark and dying world, we are successful...and completely so.

Lord willing, He will use these faithful proclamations to bring about the changes that we so desperately need and desire, but that is for Him and Him alone to decide. Our mission is simple faithfulness; faithfulness to proclaim what He has commanded and equipped us to proclaim while having faith that He will honor that obedience perfectly according to His perfect will and plan, rather than our own.

This approach to politics and political conversations and political solutions will instantly bring us into conflict with many secularly obsessed, pragmatism obsessed folks, including most of those in the Republican Establishment.

They will do everything that they can to get us to bite - as we have every time in the past - on Christ-less solutions to every social, moral, and economic problem that we are facing at this pivotal moment in American history.

One of the hopes and goals of this book is to equip Christ-honoring readers to simply, thoroughly, and unapologetically, dismiss all of the same old man-centered political machinations that have led the nation and culture into its current wild chase after the judgment of the righteous, holy God whom we serve.

The essential truths of the Gospel and Christ's revealed nature cannot be compromised. Not in the political realm or anywhere else.

We are called to proclaim His Gospel to all and exalt His lordship over all. When we actually submit to that call, He may - just may - save an otherwise unsalvageable nation.

That is our only hope.

He is our only hope.

And our simple obedience to Him is the only path to that hope.

GOD BLESS AMERICA...WITH REPENTANCE

*We destroy arguments and every lofty opinion raised against the knowledge of God, and **take every thought captive to obey Christ***

2 CORINTHIANS 10:5

For I am not ashamed of the gospel, for it is the power of God for salvation to everyone who believes

ROMANS 1:16

It is important to repent not only of specific, externally visible sins or patterns or even thoughts. It is also essential that we repent of having believed false ideas or bought into false concepts...such as there being a Christ-less solution to...well...*anything*.

The American Way has been so thoroughly separated from anything explicitly Christ-centered that the average American - even the average American professing Christian or evangelical - has little problem at all supporting the notion that Christ or religion or religious beliefs can and in some cases must be separated out - set aside and prevented from "interfering" with the good and proper flow of things, be they political things or business things or personal sexual preference things or...you get the picture.

This is an evil of which we must repent and from which we must turn. The proclamation of this hard truth will be a central theme of this work as we go along, so the reader is well served to consider the centrality of this component now.

GOD GRACE AMERICA'S CHRISTIANS...WITH KINDNESS

A new commandment I give to you, that you love one another: just as I have loved you, you also are to love one another. 35 By this all people will know that you are my disciples, if you have love for one another."

JESUS (THE REAL ONE), IN JOHN 13:34-35

"If you love me, you will keep my commandments."

JESUS (THE REAL ONE), IN JOHN 14:15

Yet while we are bringing what the Bible itself describes as a matchlessly offensive, hatred-inspiring truth to a world at war with holiness and its Source, we are always to aim to present these brutal truths in the supernatural Spirit of personal humility that should define every true Christian's life. In entering into political conversations and treading into the political realm for the sake of Christ's glory, we must resist the persistent temptation to self-righteousness and hypocrisy. This too is an area in which our proper understanding of the Gospel is of great aid and comfort, for if we know that while we yet hated Him, He chose to save us and that any good thing we have or think or do is a gift from Him, then we will find ourselves leaving little room for self-centered pride or boasting...and we will shine all the more brightly in this darkened place for it.

This is the light and the heat that will set us apart. These are the things that will inspire those around us to listen and, Lord willing, repent and be saved. And when and if the Lord chooses to save enough of those people listening to enough of those Christ-centered proclamations of truth, then maybe, just maybe, America will be saved.

That result is entirely up to Him.

The obedience to proclaim His Gospel and nature throughout the world is entirely up to us. And He has perfectly equipped and called us to this task. All we need do now is obey.

Lord willing, this book will help to equip and encourage American Christians - and all Christians in all places - to do just that.

Every moral question or political issue is an opportunity. Every social question or political issue is an opportunity. Every economic question or political issue is an opportunity. Every question touched by the realm of politics is an opportunity to exalt Christ; proclaim the Gospel; shatter every idiotic, man-centered misconception; and expose every stupid elephant trick that would, in the name of secular "progress", aim to distract us from the Source of all truth and beauty.

What a honor to be chosen by Him for this mission in this place at this moment! The time is now. The command has been given. The mission is upon us.

Has Christ-less morality ever had a chance of building a truly moral culture?

Nope.

Has Christ-less economic policy of business practices ever had a chance of bringing true and lasting material prosperity to a people?

Nuh uh.

Has Christ-less "education" ever had a snowball's chance in you-know-where of bringing about anything better than a Christ-less, pro-Statist drone mentality in the masses?

Of course not.

Has Christ-less leadership in any area ever been a good, much less the best, path to greatness for a people at any time in any place for any reason?

No, no, and no.

With the core of every stupid elephant trick being the proposition that true excellence can be pursued in any area of life without the explicit proclamation of Christ as Lord and the seeking of His nature and will for ultimate guidance is sheer...well...stupidity. And it's the particular brand of stupidity that this book is aimed and exposing. And mocking. And correcting.

No more rabbits. No more rabbit trails. No more diversions or distractions. And no more stupid elephant tricks. While neither of us may be Napoleon Bonaparte, we have been infinitely better equipped for battle than he or any other man has ever been.

We are here for great purpose and the time is now to take up His banner and march to perfect victory that He has assured in His time, according to His purpose, and for His glory.

We have enemy strongholds to crush, a Kingdom to advance, and plenty of big game to hunt along the way...by His grace and for His glory...

SECTION THREE

~

Stupid Elephant Tricks

5

CONVENIENT CHRISTIANITY

THE STUPID PRAGMATISM TRICK

prag·mat·ic [prag-mat-ik]
adjective
1. of or pertaining to a practical point of view or practical considerations.[4]

*And he said to all, "If anyone would come after me, **let him deny himself and take up his cross daily and follow me**. For whoever would save his life will lose it, but whoever loses his life for my sake will save it. For what does it profit a man if he gains the whole world and loses or forfeits himself? For whoever is ashamed of me and of my words, of him will the Son of Man be ashamed when he comes in his glory and the glory of the Father and of the holy angels."*

LUKE 9:23-26 (BOLD EMPHASIS ADDED)

Let's face it: Martyrdom just isn't practical.

---

[4] Dictionary.com Unabridged
Based on the Random House Dictionary, © Random House, Inc. 2012.

It tends to wreck the whole day, and pretty much every one thereafter...at least when you define things secularly.

Who's gonna feed the dog or get the kids to school if we get all burned up at the stake and stuff, right? There's just no reasonable way to do this martyrdom thing, and besides, wouldn't it really be better for all involved if we were unmartyred and still around to help our friends, family, and church?

Obviously, perspectives such as these are thoroughly pragmatic, so long as said pragmatism is centered on one's self. In light of self-centered principles of pragmatism, self-sacrifice to such an extreme as actual God honoring martyrdom is flat out dumb.

In this we see that pragmatism - just as love, faith, reason, and hope - is only as true and good or unreliable and bad as the object upon which it is founded. In this case, secular pragmatism is objectively destructive and evil because it is man-centered, whereas God-centered pragmatism - the kind that exalts rather than bemoans things like martyrdom for the true faith - is wonderful and good because it is firmly rooted in the pursuit of God's glory over our own comfort, and even our own life.

Obviously this difference in opinions where the notion of pragmatism is concerned is a pretty big deal, and, just as obviously, the modern conservative movement in general and the contemporary Republican Party in particular have both become defined by an acute slavery to secular pragmatism.

SUPERNATURAL PRACTICALITY

And whatever you do, in word or deed, do everything in the name of the Lord Jesus, giving thanks to God the Father through him.

COLOSSIANS 3:17

"We must not suppose that if we succeeded in making everyone nice we should have saved their souls. A world of nice people, content in their own niceness, looking no further, turned away from God, would be just as desperately in need of salvation as a miserable world."

C.S. LEWIS

With events like John the Baptist's decapitation and Stephen's stoning being decidedly impractical from a secular perspective for John and Stephen, respectively, and with our being, by God's grace, firmly and completely in the same camp that John and Stephen occupy, we are well served to dwell for a moment upon just how utterly nuts our ways of defining what is reasonable or pragmatic are perceived to be from this fallen world's perspective. It's also useful for us to take something of a sustained look at our own standards of pragmatism in practice where the likes of John, Stephen, and the many other martyrs for the faith provide such powerful, purposeful examples and inspiration.

When we see John the Baptist faithful - and boldly so - unto death for the sake of the proclamation of truth, we should not only take notice, but seek to emulate such a clearly Christ-centered example. When we see Stephen proclaim truth to the powers of the world even unto his own death, we should absorb and admire his dedication with awe and wonder, of course, but we should also pray for the strength to be conformed to Christ in such a manner that we are compelled to the God-centered pragmatism of Stephen.

When we actually believe that Christ *is* Lord; the all-powerful Creator and Sustainer of all things, and that He has chosen and empowered us as His representatives here, how *practical* would it really be for us to be anything but obedient to Him, even unto our physical deaths here and now? If we chase after and grasp the beauty, truth, and power of this reality, how much less concerned with our reputations and status in the eyes of the world might be become?

How much less concerned will we be when it comes to public opinion polls or even election results if our confidence is not founded or dependent upon those results, but is rather rooted in the matchless comfort that comes through obedience to the all-powerful, perfect sovereign of the Universe?

As with so many other truths of the Christian life, our practicality and pragmatism are *supernatural* at their core and, as such, they stand in stark contrast to the ways and standards of this world.

God requires our obedience of us, not due to any need within Him, but due to the need for Him that is within us. Only when we obey Him in the most dire and otherwise hopeless of situations can we lay claim to the matchless power that He provides His people through such trials. In our submission to His will during those most challenging times, He is most glorified and we are most blessed.

This is the pragmatism to which we, by His grace, subscribe, and this is the counter-cultural, supernatural pragmatism that we are to present to the world through our faithful obedience to our perfect Lord and King.

This God-centered pragmatism, when on display in the lives - including the *political* lives - of His people, cannot help but cast the pathetic counterfeit that currently captivates the culture in a proper, revealing light. Along those lines, we have already been given enough of that light to see in some detail some of the more destructive forms of God-less pragmatism that have come to be embraced in most Republican and conservative circles.

One manifestation of the perversion of God-centered pragmatism into the man-centered sort that has become wildly popular in Republican and Tea Party circles is the "objectivism" perspective that was pioneered and advanced by Ayn Rand, the atheist author of best-selling, influential works including *The Fountainhead* and *Atlas Shrugged*. Rand, her perspectives, and their impact will be further addressed in Chapter 6.

Another form of man-centered pragmatism that we have to watch for and guard against - one that comes with a smile and fits quite comfortably for the average conservative Republican type these days - is the inclination to measure things not only by man-centered standards, but by the standard set by a single, specific man...even if that man is Ronald Reagan.

A BIGGER-THAN-REAGAN REVOLUTION

"Without God there is no virtue because there is no prompting of the conscience...without God there is a coarsening of the society; without God democracy will not and cannot long endure...If we ever forget that we are One Nation Under God, then we will be a Nation gone under."

RONALD REAGAN

"Where, oh where, is the next Ronald Reagan?"
   "What this nation needs is another Reagan!"
   "Rea-*gan!* Rea-*gan!* Rea-*gan!*"
   "Whatever will we do without him...or at least another one like him?" *sniff sniff*

"Why didn't we clone him when we had the chance?!"

In the years since George H.W. Bush's catastrophic (and gloriously *progressive*) follow-up to the brief American respite from decline known as "the Reagan years", American conservatives have become increasingly annoyed, frustrated, and downright disturbed by the powers that be in the G.O.P. and the decidedly *un*-Reagan path they've charted for the party since The Gipper finished his stint as leader of the relatively free world.

There are many intriguing questions about this stretch of recent history that stretches into the present that we are unlikely to fully grasp on this side of eternity. Why is the G.O.P. establishment so bent on avoiding Reagan-esque approaches to, well, pretty much *anything* of significance? Why is the Republican controlling elite so obsessed with propelling moderate, decidedly un-Reagan candidates to the party's Presidential nomination...again and again and again... And when exactly did the Republican establishment formally succumb to and/or embrace their present phobia of winning sweeping, landslide, blow-the-opposition-out-of-the-water national elections?

Hard to say. And we won't bother trying.

What we will do is take a look at one critical and revealing moment from the flawed but at least somewhat encouraging Reagan presidency. That moment came in the autumn of 1986 in Iceland's capital city of Reykjavik.

REAGAN, REYKJAVIK, RISK, AND REWARD

The fear of the LORD is the beginning of wisdom; all those who practice it have a good understanding. His praise endures forever!

PSALM 111:10

"Freedom prospers when religion is vibrant and the rule of law under God is acknowledged."

RONALD REAGAN

In 1986, the cold war was raging. Well, at least as much as a cold war can, anyway.

Prior to Ronald Reagan's arrival in the White House, America had seen its prior position of prominence and high regard radically diminished on all fronts. Her economy was in a tailspin; her military was gutted, demoralized, and over-extended; her people were increasingly hopeless and miserable, and they were told by their leadership that this was just the natural course of things and that Americans just needed to get used to the "new reality" of their nation's condition and place in the world.

So, basically, it was then as it is today. Pre-Reagan America was pretty much just like today's America under Barack Obama.

Within a few years of taking office, Reagan had turned around the economy, rebuilt the military, revived the American spirit (though not in an explicitly Christ-centered way, which we will focus on more later), and restored the position of prominence that the nation held in the World. And he did these things in the setting of the ongoing Cold War between the western powers led by the

United States and the Soviet empire, which dominated what was then known as the Eastern Bloc of nations.

By '86, the Reagan military recovery and build-up was in high gear, and the Soviets were, for the first time, struggling to compete with the pace of American military spending, especially on the research and development front. Of particular interest and concern to the Soviets was the United States' Strategic Defense Initiative, which was aimed at using cutting edge technologies to create what would essentially be a "shield in space" against any Soviet nuclear missile attack against America or the West.

American media dubbed the program "Star Wars" and pressure began to surge from every angle against Reagan and his "Star Wars program". The Soviets hated it (which was always a good sign), the American Left hated it (which is always a good sign), which of course meant that the American liberal establishment media - which dominated all media at the time (there was no "alternative media" or even FOX news back then) - hated it and undermined it at every turn.

As the Soviet communist government fell further behind and realized the impossibility of their competing with this new nuke-snuffing (and Soviet threat defusing) technology, the pressure mounted on Reagan to abandon this shield from Soviet aggression. In the name of peace, of course.

Reagan, always painted as a trigger happy cowboy nut job, was constantly attacked personally. He was painted as a buffoon at every turn. (Still is, as a part of basic Leftist Orthodoxy.) "Star Wars" was presented by the Soviet, American network newscasts, and the garden variety state programmed college campus drone as a threat to peace; a destabilizing force that could plunge the world into nuclear conflict, rather than make said conflict pointless for an aggressor, as advertised.

Finally, in October of 1986, a summit was held in Reykjavik, Iceland, between Reagan and Soviet leader Mikhail Gorbachev. Radical proposals had been put on the table as a result of the American return to strength and the Soviet realization that they simply could not sustain a competitive position if things continued much longer as they had since Reagan and his policies took hold in Washington. The Russians proposed to eliminate 50% of all ICBMs, all intermediate-range nuclear forces, and 50% of all other non-ICBM strategic arms. They even agreed not to include British and French weapons in the totals. They offered all of these things - concessions that would have been unimaginable just five years earlier, in exchange for just one teeny, tiny little thing: America's practical abandonment of S.D.I.

So frightening was the potential of this nuclear-arsenal-dismissing technology to the Soviets and so confident were the Russians in America's ability to actually produce this "space shield" that Gorbachev brought what he, and much of the rest of the world, believed to be an irresistible offer.

The pressure was on, and it was intense. Reagan had in Reykjavik been offered a king's ransom. His legacy would be secured as the President who achieved sweeping arms reduction the likes of which had previously been thought impossible. The American public would hail him; even the media would be somewhat happy about such a deal as this having been struck. Both personally and politically, Reagan had much to gain by taking the offer and claiming, what would have been in many significant ways, a great victory.

But he didn't. He declined the offer, the talks collapsed, and everyone from Pravda to CBS proclaimed the event a disaster, and the slipping away of the Soviet offer as nothing short of a catastrophe for America, the world, and even the galaxy. It was *that* bad.

When nearly every external impulse and pressure encouraged Reagan to take what the Russians offered, he kept his focus. He remained true. In doing so, he was able to see clearly and do what was best for America, the world, and *particularly* the Russians.

Just a few short years after the collapse of the summit in Reykjavik, the Soviet Union itself collapsed. It died. Killed by a shield.

While the seas of political thought, popular opinion, and military possibilities raged about him, Reagan held to his guiding

85

principles, and, by the grace of God, he persevered. He stood. And the Lord used that stand to change the course of human history in dramatic fashion.

JESUS CHRIST AND THE SEA PRAGMATIC

"Immediately he made the disciples get into the boat and go before him to the other side, while he dismissed the crowds. And after he had dismissed the crowds, he went up on the mountain by himself to pray. When evening came, he was there alone, but the boat by this time was a long way from the land, beaten by the waves, for the wind was against them. And in the fourth watch of the night he came to them, walking on the sea. But when the disciples saw him walking on the sea, they were terrified, and said, "It is a ghost!" and they cried out in fear. But immediately Jesus spoke to them, saying, "Take heart; it is I. Do not be afraid."

And Peter answered him, "Lord, if it is you, command me to come to you on the water." He said, "Come." So Peter got out of the boat and walked on the water and came to Jesus. But when he saw the wind, he was afraid, and beginning to sink he cried out, "Lord, save me." Jesus immediately reached out his hand and took hold of him, saying to him, "O you of little faith, why did you doubt?"

MATTHEW 14:22-31

In Peter's walk on the water, we are given a shining example of the essential nature of the centrality and primacy of Christ in the walk of the believer. We are shown in story, vivid detail just what it is that happens when we allow any distraction to remove our focus from Him.

We sink. And fast.

Every time.

This is one of the most pervasive theme's of Scripture: Men are prone to trust in themselves rather than God and they always pay a terrible price for this profoundly misplaced hope. Time and time and time again, the perfectly recorded history of man in the Word of God reveals, confirms, and again repeats this painful reality of fallen mankind's nature - past and present.

Our loving Lord has repeated this lesson because He knows that we are a forgetful people. We are prone to forget Him more and more, almost always in direct proportion to the material comfort and peace that we enjoy. And, as Republicans are so fond of reminding anyone who will listen, America is the most materially blessed nation in all of human history. So it is that we should not be surprised to find that we are at least among the most forgetful.

We trust in what we assume to be the infinite ingenuity of an American people who have proudly and defiantly walked - or *run* - away from the source of all true wisdom, knowledge, and beauty as their guide. We trust that an endless supply of printed, fictional cash will somehow, some way manage to perpetually supply our ravenous appetites, support our people's laziness and dependence, and sustain what has been for a very long time the highest material standard of living in the world, even as we watch the foundation crack and the Titanic list. We cling to an imagined American invulnerability to foreign conquest, even after the shock of 9/11.

And why do we trust in these things? Why do we, in most cases, simply close our eyes, hope for the best, and pretend?

Because we have to.

That's all we've got.

And, as the saying goes, "you work with what you've got."

So one person starts to rearrange the deck chairs, another grabs a violin, and the masses gathered on deck watching the ship sink all dutifully listen to the man telling them "nothing to see here". And at the end of the day we all dutifully (and out of perceived necessity) line up like little lemmings and pretend it's true; that everything will be okay and somehow, some way, life as we've come to know it will go on.

Where once a man-centered pragmatism was used to nudge us down this path of "reasonable", manageable, and even desirable plans and policies, the pursuit of those policies has led us to a place where we, of necessity, must ignore every flagrant, glaring rupture in the system at every level. This is the circuit that Christ-less pragmatism runs: It replaces God-centered reason with man-centered reason, thereby destroying all that is actually reasonable, and ultimately produces in its victims a desperate clinging to what we could call - and are experiencing in America, *anti*-reason.

That's where we're at. That's where Christ-less pragmatism has taken us and where it will continue to take us...each and every time. When "we the people" decide to sever ourselves from Him, and *we* become the standard setter, the law giver, and the authors (or even the contributing authors) of truth, we are charting a path not through merely potentially treacherous waters, but straight into the most dangerous iceberg imaginable. The end result of Christ-less pragmatism is always the suicide of any person or nation that chooses it.

By seeking *our* will and *our* standards and *our* path apart from Him, we have placed the ship of American state on a suicidal collision course with His unshakable truth. By seeking our freedom and our liberty and our prosperity independent of Him, we have assured our slavery, and that slavery is even now creeping upon us.

THE INSANITY OF PRAGMATISM

The fear of the LORD is the beginning of knowledge; fools despise wisdom and instruction.

PROVERBS 1:7

"We have no government armed with power capable of contending with human passions unbridled by morality and religion. Avarice, ambition, revenge, or gallantry, would break the strongest cords of our Constitution as a whale goes through a net. Our Constitution was made only for a moral and religious people. It is wholly inadequate to the government of any other."

JOHN ADAMS

Ever notice how words and phrases have often come to mean something close to the exact opposite of what they actually, originally meant? By way of example, the concepts of "public service" and that of the "gentleman's club" both contort once noble terms for the purpose of giving participants in perversion a sort of cover. The number of truly servant-minded folks holding high office does seem roughly equivalent to the number of actual gentlemen to be found in a "gentlemen's club".

"Public servants" now routinely enjoy salaries and benefits packages that radically outpace those of their private sector counterparts (these private sector folks being the ones *paying* for those relatively gaudy "public servant" lifestyles.) And to refer to a gathering of males to watch women strip and dance for them as a "gentleman's club" is a true crime against virtue, honor, and decency. These ends-justify-the-means linguistic perversions reveal much about the character of the nation and its people, of course, but it's the pragmatic motivation for these perversions that we should take a moment to consider here.

The everyday pervasive perversion of such concepts such as what it means to serve ("service") and what it means to be a gentleman ("gentleman's club") is a direct result of a secularly pragmatic mindset taking hold and directing the way we paint and promote the things that we desire. When we also understand that if we have a Christ-less approach to life, we will have Christ-less desires, it should come as no surprise that we would use inherently destructive and perverse means in order to pursue those desires. When our desires and goals are self-centered and Christ-less, we will twist, spin, and contort in any manner we deem necessary to cover for and justify our perversions. This is the "ends justify the means" mindset at the root of pragmatism.

Of course, this is only a destructive thing because of the end in question, that being the will of fallen, rebellious man. When man-centeredness is the motivating standard and ultimate goal, the means by which that goal is pursued will be as corrupt as the goal itself. As Scripture reveals, the nature of fallen man is evil. He is born with a spirit of death, a heart of stone, he hates holiness, and he loves sin. Such a creature is incapable of producing a good sort of pragmatism.

It is only when man is reborn through the supernatural imposition of God's grace in their life that they can begin to think pragmatically from a biblically sound perspective - a sort of pragmatic thought that is as opposed to secular pragmatism as are the secular and Christian understanding of terms like "service" and "gentleman".

Since pragmatism is ultimately just a strain of the ends-justify-the-means virus, it should come as no surprise that language has been deconstructed and perverted throughout the American culture. Words are simply seen as a means by which an end is to be sold. Whether the end in question is an economic policy, the advocacy of a particular lifestyle, or the "hope" and "change" of the new progressive Marxist movement, it has and will continue to be sold through the redefinition and subsequent use of the highest, happiest terms than can be claimed and corrupted for the cause.

In this relentless pursuit of the redefinition of terms in order to accommodate the progressive desire to turn the world on its head, we have been left with a pragmatically destroyed language. Nothing can be trusted. Every political speech is assumed to be deceptive. Every promise is assumed to be empty. Every ad has an asterisk (or ten).

And we all play along, hoping, again, that somehow, some way, the pragmatic path that's led us to the brink of cultural collapse and national disaster will manage to produce salvation. If we just keep doing the same destructive thing, great good will come of it.

That belief, as they say, is the definition of insanity.

THE TYRANNY OF PRAGMATISM

"Those people who will not be governed by God will be ruled by tyrants."

WILLIAM PENN

"Democracy is two wolves and a lamb voting on what to have for lunch. Liberty is a well-armed lamb contesting the vote."

BENJAMIN FRANKLIN

While Christ-less pragmatism always leads to the suicide of any person, culture or nation snared in its embrace, it should come as no surprise that America's pragmatic path is even now making its way to a place of governmental tyranny. This is the natural course for natural man in his rebellion against the Author of truth and beauty on a national scale. When men will not be ruled by the perfect truth and loving law of God, they will be ruled by the oppressive hand of the secularly pragmatic tyrant.

This looming American reality will be covered in more detail later, but it is worth noting here the incredibly *pragmatic* nature of the never-ending, ever-growing, perpetually increasing in power type of government by which we are now afflicted.

How many new government power grabs and programs are sold with the "do it for the children" line? How many new system slaves are created by design under the banners of secularly defined compassion and thoughtfulness? The "land of the free and the home of the brave" now submits to its ruling elite on matters spanning everything from   the amount of water used by a flushing toilet. Where once Americans were known for their fierce devotion to liberty, justice, truth, and their Author, we are now rightly seen as the pathetic, cowering little brats that we have largely become.

We have embraced slavery in the name of liberty. We have exchanged truth for lies. And so profound is our denial and self-delusion that we actually wonder why we are now seeing the prosperity, peace, and power of the American past slip away. We are blinded by our warped sense of invulnerability and entitlement, and in our blindness we do not see the cleansing tidal wave that is even now cresting over the horizon, racing to our shores - shores left unprepared for this coming truth by the soft tyranny of today and the more serious version that now seems inevitable barring the supernatural intervention of the God whose wrath we have so eagerly pursued.

We are a fat, lazy, ignorant, dependant and very, very proud people. In other words, we are a tyrant's *dream*.

Yet that tyrannical dream need not continue. By God's grace, we have been equipped with all that we need to turn tyranny away and return to the matchless beauty, peace, prosperity and joy that can once again, Lord willing, light the way of the America that Ronald Reagan so often referred to as "The shining city on the hill".

GOD HAS *CLEARLY* SPOKEN

"If we abide by the principles taught in the Bible, our country will go on prospering and to prosper; but if we and our posterity neglect its instruction and authority, no man can tell how sudden a catastrophe may overwhelm us and bury all our glory in profound obscurity."

DANIEL WEBSTER

"I have wondered at times what the Ten Commandments would have looked like if Moses had run them through the US Congress."

RONALD REAGAN

We believe in America far more than we believe in God; particularly the specific God of Christianity. We believe in our "can do" spirit far more than we believe in the Spirit of the God of Christianity. We believe that we will be just fine in the end so long as we trust in our inherent goodness as Americans, rather than repenting of our failures as a people and placing our trust wholly on God the Son, Jesus Christ.

These are the truths that we must face, and change. There is no half-measure that will do; Christ must be explicitly exalted in every troubled realm that we wish to see lose its troubled status.

So long as our pragmatism is man-centered, we are doomed. Only when we aim for Christ-centeredness in all things and at all times will our sense of those things - including our notion of pragmatism - be righted and become useful rather than perverted and destructive.

When we face an issue in the political realm, just as any other, we must first seek Scripture and, most importantly, *submit* to what we there find.

Truth is not ours to author or revise. It is His, and it is all completely His. He is its source and His glorification is its ultimate goal. Our congressmen and senators and presidents may imagine for their brief moment of power as God has given it to them that they are in some way in a position to redefine truth. We see this attitude throughout the contemporary American government, and not just on the judiciary. We see elected officials of all sorts, shapes, sizes, and status go about the business of imagining and acting as though they have the power to shape truth. Happens all the time. And it fails every time it's tried.

It fails because all *true* truth is God's. It is of Him. It is entirely His possession as it is entirely an expression of His perfect character. As such it is rooted in and defined by holiness. His holiness.

By His grace and for His purposes, He has made His truth known to us in His perfect Word. He has answered *every* essential question with which we now wrestle.

What has God told us about government?

What has God told us about good and bad leadership?

What has God told us about the sanctity of life?

What has God told us about private property?

What has God told us about manhood and womanhood?

What has God told us about family

What has God told us about marriage?

What has God told us about economics?

What has god told us about charity?

What has God told *America* about life, liberty, and the pursuit of happiness?

I know, I know...we can't go there! Not publically, at least, and not publicly in a loud, consistent, and emphatic manner, to be sure. No way! What chance would we have? What would people think?

C'mon, be reasonable. Be realistic. Be *pragmatic!*

And to that we ought to say, oh yes...we agree....pragmatism is a wonderful thing, and we encourage it wholeheartedly...so long as it is completely and explicitly centered on Jesus Christ.

PRAGMATIC REFORMATION
(OR: THE REFORMATION OF PRAGMATISM)

The natural person does not accept the things of the Spirit of God, for they are folly to him, and he is not able to understand them because they are spiritually discerned. The spiritual person judges all things, but is himself to be judged by no one. "For who has understood the mind of the Lord so as to instruct him?" But we have the mind of Christ.

1 CORINTHIANS 2:14-16

"It cannot be emphasized too strongly or too often that this great nation was founded, not by religionists, but by Christians; not on religions, but on the Gospel of Jesus Christ. For this very reason peoples of other faiths have been afforded asylum, prosperity, and freedom of worship here."

PATRICK HENRY

Remember the earlier referenced phrase: "You work with what you've got."

Well, what we've "got" is *perfection!*

His perfection.

By the grace of God, we as His supernaturally adopted sons and daughters have the very Spirit of God within us. It is this Spirit that enables us to do what was previously impossible in our fallen, lost state. We have the capacity and have been given the command to seek and pursue the mind of Christ in all things. Our trust in Him is our guide. Our confidence in Him is our strength. Our assurance that He is completely sovereign is the source of our good and proper and explicitly Christ-centered *pragmatism*.

When we wonder about the legitimacy of the homosexual lifestyle, we need not wonder long. When we wonder about the definition or significance of marriage, we need not wonder long.

He *has* spoken, and clearly, on each and every essential question and truly critical issue of the day, providing each and every answer that we need. And that's where true and good pragmatism will be found - in our desire for and submission to His perfectly revealed truth.

This truth only leads to Him, and so it can only do us good.

The question we must always ask when we consider anything - political or otherwise, is: What has God said about this? Only then, and only after seeking to find and submit to what He has said, will we be equipped and able to discern and act rightly. And the more we do this, the more natural it will become.

When our guiding impulse becomes the pursuit of conformity to Christ, our reflexive responses will change. Our lives will change. Our culture will change - a little or a lot, and all according to His will.

His will is to become our own, and if that is to happen, we must seek to discover what His will is. As we pursue this sanctifying walk, by His grace and for His glory, we will shape and cultivate a biblically sound pragmatism - a pragmatism centered on Him and not on us; on His will and not our own.

And with that view of pragmatism and a desire for His will and glory firmly in mind, let's move on to an examination of another perverted notion that has grown popular among the Republican faithful...a perversion we will call the Stupid Libertarian Trick...

6

GIVE ME LIBERTY AND GIVE ME DEATH

THE STUPID LIBERTARIAN TRICK

lib·er·tar·i·an [lib-er-tair-ee-uhn]
noun
1. a person who advocates liberty, especially with regard to thought or conduct.[5]

Stand fast therefore in the liberty wherewith Christ hath made us free, and be not entangled again with the yoke of bondage.

GALATIANS 5:1 (KJV)

"It is when people forget God that tyrants forge their chains."

PATRICK HENRY

---

[5] Dictionary.com Unabridged
Based on the Random House Dictionary, © Random House, Inc. 2012.

"You can get it in any color you want, as long as it's red."

This early '90s announcement regarding the much anticipated production of the high-end, supercool new (and much needed) image car for the Chrysler corporation, the Dodge Viper, was an echo of Ford's approach as taken in the earliest days of the mass produced automobile when the Model T was first offered up "in any color you want, so long as it's black.".

Of course, the Viper was *so* powerful and *so* beautiful and *so* captivating in the eyes of its target audience that a little thing like a "red only" color choice spectrum hardly mattered at all. It looked great in red, and, as we all know, red is faster.

Sometime after the announcement of the "red only" restriction and the actual availability of Vipers for purchase, the limitation faded and faded from consideration to the point that Vipers were just red. Red was what they were. And wasn't that a good thing? Red is faster, after all.

So the fast and flashy new Vipers flew off of showroom floors almost as fast as they could be rolled off the assembly line. The freedom to buy a Viper in any color, so long as it was red, was clearly a hit. Dodge was happy. Parent company Chrysler was happy. Auto enthusiasts were happy. New Viper owners were happy. And police seeking a bump in speeding ticket revenue for their budget crunched localities were happy. Everybody won.

Few Viper owners cared about the limited choice of color. Most didn't even notice. And practically everyone thought the end result was very, very cool, so why rock the boat?

Obviously, Dodge was free to produce the car in other colors (and later would), and potential customers were free to buy or support or not buy and not support the product. This is the nature of a free market.

But that market, like the concepts of freedom and liberty itself, is radically impacted in its functionality and fundamentally defined in its character by its relationship to the one and only source of all truth, beauty, and goodness: The Lord Jesus Christ.

LIBERTY IN THE LAND OF THE DEAD

Do you not know that all of us who have been baptized into Christ Jesus were baptized into his death? We were buried therefore with him by baptism into death, in order that, just as Christ was raised from the dead by the glory of the Father, **we too might walk in newness of life***.*

ROMANS 6:3-4 (BOLD EMPHASIS ADDED)

And **you were dead in the trespasses and sins in which you once walked, following the course of this world***, following the prince of the power of the air, the spirit that is now at work in the sons of disobedience— among whom we all once lived in the passions of our flesh, carrying out the desires of the body and the mind, and were by nature children of wrath, like the rest of mankind.* **But God, being rich in mercy, because of the great love with which he loved us, even when we were dead in our trespasses, made us alive together with Christ***—by grace you have been saved— and raised us up with him and seated us with him in the heavenly places in Christ Jesus, so that in the coming ages he might show the immeasurable riches of his grace in kindness toward us in Christ Jesus. For by grace you have been saved through faith.* **And this is not your own doing; it is the gift of God, not a result of works, so that no one may boast.** *For we are his workmanship, created in Christ Jesus for good works, which God prepared beforehand, that we should walk in them.*

EPHESIANS 2:1-10 (BOLD EMPHASIS ADDED)

Biblically, we know that every unconverted, unrepentant, unbelieving man or woman walking or ever to have walked the earth is free to choose their liberty or their freedom in any color that they like. And that color will always be black.

It will always be black because it will always be Christ-less. It will be totally black, totally bleak, and freely chosen by the unconverted each and every time. That's how human nature works and that's why a *super*natural solution is necessary.

Just as with secular pragmatism, secular libertarianism must first, foremost, and always be seen in light of its explicit *Christlessness*. Before we even begin to examine the merits or weaknesses of any offshoot or consequence of the secular Libertarian worldview in practice, we must grab hold of the truth that, however practical (or *pragmatic*) it may appear and however many attractive benefits it may offer, in its purposeful resistance to the proclamation of Christ as Lord over all, secular Libertarianism is incurably burdened with a satanic/anti-Christian core.

Obviously, that's a big deal.

Also a big deal is our recognition of the fact that, until we who are Christians were supernaturally saved by a holy God while we still hated Him and His holiness, we were once bound to a sinful nature and would always freely and happily choose to embrace Christ-less philosophies, worldviews, and ways of life. That's how *we* were once wired, so patience is in order here. We were once unconverted, God-hating rebels, each and every one of us, and it is in this light that a great opportunity presents itself: We have been graced with the chance to *love others as Christ has loved us* - by firmly and lovingly proclaiming truth - often hard and unpopular truth - in a Spirit of grace and kindness that transcends natural human understanding, all by His grace and for His glory. And as many of you reading, like the author, have something of a Libertarian streak, we should have less trouble than usual attaching the very appropriate "there but by the grace go I" tag to this subject.

Liberty is a beautiful thing....

...and truth is a beautiful thing...

...only insofar as they are explicitly and wholly founded upon Christ.

Apart from Christ, all *apparently* or once good things become fundamentally corrupt and inexorably destructive. Corrupted liberty and corrupted freedom are no exceptions. If anything, they are prime examples of corrupted beauties with the power to destroy and enslave to sin on a wide scale.

This vital Christ-centered line of demarcation has been intentionally obscured to the point of invisibility by the secular Libertarian movement. This is the line we will revisit, redraw, and reinforce in this chapter and, as we do so, Lord willing, some of us might just find good cause for personal reconsideration, repentance, and restoration.

THE MYTH (AND DANGER) OF CHRIST-LESS LIBERTY

"Bad men cannot make good citizens. A vitiated state of morals, a corrupted public conscience are incompatible with freedom."

PATRICK HENRY

"If I am the vine; you are the branches. Whoever abides in me and I in him, he it is that bears much fruit, for **apart from me you can do nothing**."

JESUS (THE REAL ONE) IN JOHN 15:5
(BOLD EMPHASIS ADDED)

The unconverted are bound by their very natures to *always* freely choose that which is self-centered over that which is Christ-centered. Nobody - God included - "makes them do" that which they do not personally desire to do. The reality is that all unconverted people always desire self-centeredness (sin) and abhor Christ-centeredness (holiness) until and unless the very God that they hate chooses, by His grace, to personally, supernaturally intervenes in their life, fundamentally changing their nature in the process. Their will then freely follows their new nature, just as it did the old.

It's not that people aren't free to choose; they are completely free to choose. The problem that requires a supernatural intervention is the problem of man's very nature - something than man himself cannot change. It is simply who he is. All born "of Adam" are, by nature, capable of choosing only from the options that their nature acknowledges as attractive and available. As Scripture tells us, the unregenerate cannot see, much less choose, the Kingdom of God. The free will is always a slave to the nature, and just as the nature of Christians is that of a New Creature, supernaturally reborn and transformed by His grace and for His keeping, so too is the nature of the unbeliever defined by its inherent darkness, love of sin, and aversion to holiness. This is why Scripture so often speaks of people as either being slaves to sin or slaves to Christ. All are born slaves to sin. All who are supernaturally reborn from above are reborn as slaves to Christ. We are all slaves of one or the other. There is no third ground, no middle of the road, or in-between condition. There are two camps. No more. No less.

The counterintuitive thing about these camps, at least from a secular or uninformed perspective, is that they are filled with happy, willing inhabitants. Happy slaves. Really.

So when a non-Christian is given liberty, he will always choose self-serving, self-centeredness. And happily so. When a non-Christian is given freedoms, he will always use those freedoms to pursue self-centered goals. And happily so. And the more of both he's given, the more selfishness he will pursue...all very happily so.

This is the danger and power of Christ-less Libertarianism.

The desire to freely pursue self-centered material pursuits apart from Christ is no good thing. It is always evil and always leads to destruction, no matter how much material wealth is secured or how much material prosperity is temporarily attained (and it is all so very temporary).

The desire to freely pursue self-centered pleasures apart from Christ is no good thing. It too is always evil and always leads to destruction, no matter how many sensuous experiences are attained in this fleeting, temporal lifetime.

The pursuit of liberty and freedom for the sake of liberty and freedom for one's self or for a group of people, large or small, apart from Christ is not a good thing. Not at all. It is evil. And it will always lead to destruction and despair, as we see all across the smoldering cultural wasteland that defines the modern day United States, a nation self-consecrated to the relentless pursuit of self-serving liberty and self-serving freedom, no matter where those self-serving impulses lead.

Liberty and freedom are only as good as the object upon which they are founded. Like faith, they are only as good as the object in whose hands and by whose standards they are held. When they are man- and self-centered, they are dark. When Christ-centered, they are light and they are good.

As with all things, motive and inspiration are the key to understanding and interpreting the actions and pursuits of men. It's all a matter of the heart in the end, and a heart that is spiritually dead and adoring of sin (self-centeredness) will never choose to submit to God or pursue holiness. Only the supernaturally regenerated new creature with the new nature and the new "heart of flesh" that replaces his of "heart of stone" can and will always seek to submit to God and pursue holiness. Only can a New Creature in Christ make God glorifying good use of liberty and freedom, and the only way for a dead spiritual person to be supernaturally reborn into such a New Creature is through the proclamation of the Gospel, so no matter how practical or tempting or comfortable or nice it may seem to share the many things we might well appreciate in concert with our Libertarian-minded friends

Our repeated recognition and awareness of these truths is essential to a proper understanding of liberty, freedom, and secular

Libertarianism. And when we fully embrace God's clearly revealed truth regarding the nature of all of humanity as willing, happy slaves to the world or willing, happy slaves to Christ that we will more and more recognize the necessity and appreciate the reality of God's perfect, gracious, supernatural solution.

The clear revelation of man's depraved nature in the Word of God is one of those areas radically misunderstood - and often times flatly denied - by many a prominent proponent of Libertarianism or Conservatism. This "missing of the fundamental point", whether intentional or not, has been a great contributor to the advancement of secular Libertarianism. No less a conservative icon than Ronald Reagan himself has become well known - and oft praised - for his advocacy of the notion that men are inherently good.

While, by God's grace, Reagan may have been good, and even good for America, that same God has made it plain that unconverted man is, by nature, evil. As uncomfortable a reality as this may be, it must be understood. As unpopular a reality as this may be, it must be proclaimed, for it is an essential component of the only supernatural weapon with which we have to advance the cause of true liberty and true freedom: The whole, undiluted Gospel of Jesus Christ.

LIBERTY'S RESURRECTION
(OR: THE REFORMATION OF LIBERTARIANISM)

Jesus said to him, "I am the way, and the truth, and the life. No one comes to the Father except through me."

JOHN 14:6

"If you abide in my word, you are truly my disciples, and you will know the truth, and the truth will set you free."

JESUS (THE REAL ONE) IN JOHN 8:32-33

Where secular Libertarianism aims to "liberate" the very concepts of truth, liberty, and freedom from any explicitly Christ-centered foundation, we are called and equipped to refute this error and proclaim the essential reality of Christ as Lord over all.

Our primary means of winning converts to this cause, however, does not center on our refutations of misconceptions, our correction of perverted political views, or our clever arguments and articulate presentation. It isn't even the "good life" that can be produced in people - Pagan and otherwise - through obedience to many of the pronouncements made by God in His Word.

We can argue for any number of good and proper political and cultural positions and changes, but what we must understand is that, while those cases made and won may produce, for a brief time, a positive shift on the margins in the land, as it did during the Reagan years, these positions and changes cannot and will not save a single person. They have not that power. And if a family or a community or a nation is comprised of unsaved people merely practicing good works for self-serving reasons rather than for

Christ-centered ones, they are ultimately doomed. they are doomed both here and eternally - here in the form of their children or grandchildren enduring the inevitable plunge from temporal peace and prosperity that is always born of man-centered pursuits and approached to government, and later - eternally - in the Christ-less forever that always follows a Christ-less earthly life.

So the stakes here are much higher than those closely associated with unemployment rates, poverty rates, and other measures of material life and success. The stakes are infinitely higher than that. They are of eternal significance and the stupid elephant tricks of self-centered pragmatism and self-centered libertarianism have almost completely succeeded in distracting us from this critical truth.

Does the unemployment rate in America matter?

Yes! It certainly does.

Do the rate of inflation, the devaluation of the dollar, and that dollar's looming loss of its world standard status each pose a serious threat to the financial health of each and every American?

Absolutely.

Does the legal murder of over a million innocent children for the sake of convenience each year for decades and counting warrant the attention of the people of a nation chasing this hard after the wrath of a just and holy God?

You bet it does.

But none of these issues and none of the discussion of these issues, however much they may positively, temporarily impact the culture, will save a single soul. And until a person is supernaturally saved, they simply will not persistently pursue rightness or righteousness. They will not because their nature will not allow it. Their every choice will be self-centered.

Only through the Gospel can a person be saved, so even, and especially, in the political realm, if we wish to see real, lasting beauty, peace, prosperity and joy take and hold root where now we have such ugliness, despair, poverty, and darkness, we must make the Gospel not only a part of our political view, but its centerpiece.

We haggle over temporal wealth, power, and politics until the cows come home, but until and unless we completely refute the contemporary, pragmatic approach to chasing liberty, freedom, and truth apart from the Author of true liberty, freedom, and truth, we are doomed to chase our tails around an enemy-designed track of distraction - a grand rabbit trail, you might say. In doing so, we willfully consign future generations - our children - to a very dark , more-Orwellian-than-*1984* future.

Christ and His Gospel must define and inform our every political view. Christ is our liberty. Christ is our freedom. We cannot advance the cause of either of these beautiful created concepts without explicitly proclaiming and advancing the name and nature of their Author. And as we faithfully obey our Lord's command to proclaim His hard and true Gospel to the lost, we will, Lord willing finally, and formidably, find more and more and more born again new creatures taking up His banner, proclaiming His liberty, and living His freedom. Then, and only then, America might be saved.

If we can manage to avoid the countless rabbit trails of distractions that define the modern political landscape and remain focused on Christ and the cross, countless opportunities will make themselves plain. When we are faithful and prepared, He will always give us the opportunity to demonstrate our faith and use what He has given us. When He gives us these moments, we must seize them. All for Him.

Do we need to know, in great detail, the history and evolution of the political and philosophical theories and thoughts that have evolved and intersected to form modern day American Libertarianism?

Nope. Hardly. (and *whew!*)

Do we need to know the latest Libertarian positions or trends, the current Libertarian Party platform, or the coming campaign schedule of Ron Paul?

Not at all.

All we need know in order to discuss all of the things that matter most where the subjects of liberty, freedom, and truth are concerned is their Author and what He has made plain on the subjects. The Word made flesh is the perfect Word that we can rely upon perfectly to form our thoughts on these matters so that we are more than able to share pertinent, insightful ideas on each of them while leading each and every conversation to its ultimate objective: The glorification of God through our submission to Christ in the proclamation of His Gospel. That supernatural Gospel can and will effectively change the very nature of His chosen people, and in doing so it will inevitably reform their notion of liberty and their notion of freedom. The truth, Christ, will set them free - free to know and proclaim the perfect freedom, liberty, and truth that they have found in Him, by His grace and for His glory.

That's the progress we aim to promote. That's the hope we have to offer. That's the change we hold in the power of His Gospel.

Libertarianism lends itself to scores of wonderful opportunities to share that Gospel.

The nature of freedom...

The nature of liberty...

The nature of slavery...

The nature of responsibility...

The nature of tyranny...

These and other central, profoundly significant subjects lay at the heart of Libertarianism and at the heart of Christianity. They providentially intersect in many places and at many levels, and we ought seize every opportunity made possible through those intersections while there is yet time.

For our unsaved Libertarian friends, we have only one hope: Christ. We have only one saving message: His Gospel. We can and must offer these matchless gems at every opportunity in a Spirit of true grace and love - love sometimes being a very hard thing and requiring that very hard things be addressed.

To our Brothers and Sisters in Christ who subscribe to a brand of secular Libertarianism, we must kindly, graciously, and patiently direct or redirect them to Christ and the cross. We must encourage and celebrate with them the beautiful necessity of proclaiming Christ as Lord of all. In this, by His grace, we might win them not to our specific place, position, or view, but His.

By keeping Him as the center of all things - including liberty- and freedom- extolling political conversations, He will be glorified. And isn't that all that really matters?

So this chapter ends as it began, and as the last chapter began and ended as well: With the bad news of warped modern ideas regarding liberty and freedom overwhelmed by the good news of the Gospel of Christ, the Author and Sustainer of true liberty and true freedom for His people, by His grace, and for His glory.

EMPIRE BUILDING FOR DUMMIES
THE STUPID NEO-CON TRICK

ne·o·con·serv·a·tism [nee-oh-kuhn-sur-vuh-tiz-uhm]
noun
moderate political conservatism   espoused or advocated by former liberals or socialists.[6]

They promise them freedom, but they themselves are slaves of corruption. For whatever overcomes a person, to that he is enslaved.

2 PETER 2:19

"No protracted war can fail to endanger the freedom of a democratic country."

ALEXIS DE TOCQUEVILLE

"We have always been at war with Eastasia."

---

[6] Dictionary.com Unabridged
Based on the Random House Dictionary, © Random House, Inc. 2012.

GEORGE ORWELL, *1984*

Well whaddaya know? We're about to attack another country. Again. And right after attacking another country. Again. And you know what we were just before we attacked *that* country? You guessed it...we were "protecting Democracy" and/or "spreading Democracy" at gunpoint in yet another distant land. It's getting to the point where news of a new American attack/invasion somewhere might be reasonably expected to reflexively produce something like an "Oh, is it Wednesday again already?" response. That's just how weirdly normal this whole American invasion thing has become. But maybe none of this should be surprising. After all, we have *always* been at war with Eastasia and/or terror, right?

If the formal governments of nations can be said to have hobbies, the modern progressive American government's favorite is clearly invading and attacking places. Lots of places. All for the cause of "liberty and freedom", of course...and liberty and freedom being *secularly* defined, of course. This is where our earlier touched upon notions of *God*-centered freedom and liberty become essential to our further contemplation of America's present and future as currently charted by the progressive powers that be atop the Republican Party and, to a great extent, at the wheel of the power structure that is the American government. As in earlier chapters, we will consider and focus upon a few critical points and aim to inspire a God-centered approach to the resolution of the subject matter they address by asking questions that "the powers that be" tend not to want asked. If we really do believe that Christ is Lord of all, then we must aim to know and seek after His will where our military policies and pursuits are concerned, however uncomfortable or challenging it may initially be to do so.

There was a time when we *might* have credibly claimed ignorance, at least in the eyes of men. There was a time when we might have assumed some sort of true (as in: God-centered) virtue or goodness in our military structure and the practices of the Pentagon. There was a time when a naiveté born largely of ignorance might have been justifiable. But, by the grace of God, *that time has passed.*

We have been called and equipped to know, defend, and advance *true* freedom and *true* liberty through the true Gospel of Christ. It is now time that we actively, eagerly seek His will - explicitly - before it is too late and a dying America becomes a dead one. As we consider the approach that we, as Christian people comprising a portion of America (a portion blessed with His grace and a portion therefore more responsible in His eyes), are taking to our military involvement with and occupation of much of the world, we must seek to know, above all else, Is what we are doing pleasing to Him? And we cannot answer that question accurately by appealing to our standards (secularly pragmatic and man-centered), but only by appealing and submitting to *His* standards (God-centered and *completely* in sync with His perfect Word).

Being pro-America can be a good and beautiful thing. Being pro American military can be just as wonderful and right. But these things, as all others, are only good insofar as they are in submission and conformity to the clear will of God. As they deviate from this, they become darker and darker, until they arrive at the point of complete severance from Him and, in doing so, place themselves in a place of total darkness. This is the darkness we must seek to avoid when possible, repent of when necessary, and combat as all times. We are strangers in a strange land; pilgrims in a foreign country. This world is not our home. This truth must be held close and dear, lest we roll with the tide of any tradition or patriotism that would entice us to place anything - America included - above Him.

The most pro-America thing we can do is encourage her to be more Christ-like; to submit to Him and find the true liberty, peace, prosperity, and joy that was once her promise. The most pro-military thing we can do is encourage it to do the same. If we believe Him, we believe these things, and if we believe these things, we will live them...even when the entire culture has been mobilized for perpetual progressive war.

WOOHOO! IT'S WAR-PREPAGANDA TIME!

"It is well that war is so terrible. We should grow too fond of it."

ROBERT E. LEE

"Everyone then who hears these words of mine and does them will be like a wise man who built his house on the rock. And the rain fell, and the floods came, and the winds blew and beat on that house, but it did not fall, because it had been founded on the rock. And **everyone who hears these words of mine and does not do them will be like a foolish man who built his house on the sand. And the rain fell, and the floods came, and the winds blew and beat against that house, and it fell, and great was the fall of it.**"

JESUS (THE REAL ONE) IN MATTHEW 7:24-27
(BOLD EMPHASIS ADDED)

I remember as a kid watching President Reagan's announcement that we had just bombed Libya. Operation El Dorado Canyon was a response to the 1986 bombing of a Berlin discotheque frequented by American military personnel. The bombing had been traced back to a Libyan dictator Muammar Gaddafi.

From all that was known at the time, and is known now, the attack was reasonable and justifiable, even to most who disagreed with it in its specifics. And this was the sort of thing that progressive media types used to paint President Reagan as a dangerous, trigger-happy yahoo, just one finger itch away from plunging the world into nuclear holocaust.

116

Fast forward to 2012, and we see a very progressive Democrat President, Barack Obama, supervising a seemingly assembly line approach to war-mongering throughout the Middle East, including, you guessed it, Libya. Where Reagan had to overcome an opposition media, Obama's never-ending war machine enjoys the support of the progressive movement, media wings included.

At this writing, war with Iran seems to be nearly inevitable. The media has been mobilized (again). Troops are soon to follow (again). Before the troops roll and the jets fly, public opinion is being dutifully nudged into the "right" position by the media mobilization of the moment...again. The looming conflict with Iran comes on the heels of recent American military involvement in Libya. And Afghanistan. And Iraq.

The age of American Empire is upon us. It is upon the world. The American military, shaped by an ethic purged of all explicit fidelity to the God of Scripture, and funded by a currency long detached from anything of objective, transcendent value, has been sent to the four corners of the world for the purpose of, as many a good Republican will tell you, "spreading Democracy". Or "spreading freedom". Or "spreading liberty". Or, in more appreciably simple moments, just plain ol' "killing our enemies".

While each of these terms and concepts have served to carry and cover for seemingly infinite amounts of baggage over recent years of American intervention, there is, for the first time in memory, a building sense among many Christians that something is wrong here. Something *very* wrong. The media war-prepaganda has lost its savor. The drumbeat is proving less inspiring. This would seem to be a refreshing display of discernment on the part of some Americans, and the time has come for us to turn the corner from questioning the statist/globalist party line that has come to define American policy, and begin to openly challenge it...first with questions.

While it is far more accurate to say that the purposes of such rampant American military intervention and occupation center more on stretching the American people and economy beyond the point of no return where their own sustainability is concerned, so that something better and new might soon formally replace the current veneer of an American system, we will not be exploring those concerns in detail here. There are many good sources for such information and pursuits to be found elsewhere, and the reader is encouraged to seek them out.

There is much that has been written and much that still could be said regarding the detailed realities and consequences of the modern American Empire model, but, in an effort to maintain a God-centered approach to the contemplation of the issues covered herein, we aim at simply considering - *seriously considering* - three specific questions:

1. Is our military built upon and committed to exalting God?

2. Are our military endeavors aimed, in any explicit way, at glorifying the God of Scripture?

3. Is our international policy explicitly God-centered or explicitly man-centered?

As you might imagine, questions such as these are wildly unpopular...both with those on the left and those on the right. The Progressive Left would rather you not talk about God so much, and the Progressive Right, true to form, is okay with you talking about God, so long as you don't actually drag him into subjects like these.

And remember: We, as Christians, set apart and saved from a dying world, have no excuses. We have no out. We must face these questions seriously and honestly if we are to seek His will and be conformed to it.

Painful medicine, I know. But if He - His nature, His word, His will - really is the only source of every true solution to every problem, then we must seek Him in all things and, no matter the price or persecution, we must submit to Him and proclaim that others do the same.

WAR AND PEACE AND GRACE

To the pure, all things are pure, but to the defiled and unbelieving, nothing is pure; but both their minds and their consciences are defiled. They profess to know God, but they deny him by their works. They are detestable, disobedient, unfit for any good work.

TITUS 1:15-16

What do you have that you did not receive? If then you received it, why do you boast as if you did not receive it?

1 CORINTHIANS 4:7

Here again it is important that we demonstrate grace and avoid the ever-present temptation to self-righteousness and hypocrisy. Here we have yet another opportunity to bring truth to our world - our America - in a Spirit of true love.

Each of us have believed wrong things. We have done wrong things. And we have not been convinced or convicted of their rightness until He has opened our eyes. So it is that, while the critique here of any God-less (or God minimizing) approach to militarism or nationalism or anything else is indeed necessary and sometimes very, very hard hitting, we should always remember that this is not a call to leftists to embrace a more conservative view of things militarily, or a call to conservatives to inch a bit in a more pacifistic direction. It is nothing of the sort. It is a clear call for all who proclaim Christ as King to seek and submit to His will insofar as that will has been made plain regarding the matters of military and empire building.

The measure of all things' goodness is their reliance upon and submission to the will of God. America is no exception. America, and American Empire, are to be tested just as all other things are to be tested: In the perfect light of His perfect Word. If it is true that modern America is, as Reagan once said, "an empire of ideals", *we had best know what those ideas are* and, most importantly, be willing to test and mold them according to the perfect and sufficient guide that is Scripture.

These are the essential steps to true, God-centered American reformation, revival, and restoration.

AN AMERICA WORTH FIGHTING FOR
(OR: THE REFORMATION OF PATRIOTISM)

"The United States is unique because we are an empire of ideals."

RONALD REAGAN

"We have forgotten God. We have forgotten the gracious hand which preserved us in peace and multiplied and enriched and strengthened us, and we have vainly imagined, in the deceitfulness of our hearts, that all these blessings were produced by some superior wisdom and virtue of our own. Intoxicated with unbroken success, we have become too self-sufficient to feel the necessity of redeeming and preserving grace, too proud to pray to the God that made us."

ABRAHAM LINCOLN

I love America. I love the American military. It is assumed and expected that most, if not all, readers will share those sentiments, and it is hoped that we will all define that love by God-centered means (His Word) rather than man-centered ones (our selves, feelings, traditions, etc.).

When we understand that He raises up and crushes nations according to His purpose, and we see the current state of our own country, we must shudder...and then fall on our faces in prayer and repentance. Somewhere soon after that, having repented of having once believed such wrong things as we have in the past, we must begin to actively seek His will. And that seeking should inspire serious, open, God-centered conversations - both in the form of communion with Him through His word and prayer, and in the form of conversations with our Brothers and Sisters in Christ.

We must be willing to ask and seek, sincerely, together.

What does a God-centered military look like? What does the term even mean?

How is the manner in which our military is trained glorify God? How might it offend Him? And why might these things matter...*a lot*?

How is God glorified when we, as a nation already drowned in debt, print and heap more and more Monopoly Money upon the fire so that the engine of American progressive empire expansion might be fed?

How is it possible that this can be sustained?

How is it possible that our children will be able to endure the world we are creating through, among other things, the progressive use of the military?

Is it even *possible* to have a God-centered military or military policy, anyway?

If we are going to seek Him and His glory in all things, we have to be willing - eager, even - to tackle questions such as these, and including those three that were posed earlier in the chapter:

1. Is our military built upon and committed to exalting God?

2. Are our military endeavors aimed, in any explicit way, at glorifying the God of Scripture?

3. Is our international policy explicitly God-centered or explicitly man-centered?

The mere consideration of these subjects explicitly in this light - *His* light - is enough to warrant instant backlash and criticism from those enslaved to secular pragmatism and progressive thought - slavery of a sort that was once ours until His truth set us free. It's simply nonsensical to them, as it must be until God graces them with the eyes to see, ears to hear, and a heart to understand and love His truth.

As we consider these things and subsequently act upon what He reveals to us through those contemplations, we will then, and only then, be able to even begin to find the full answers to the questions and implement true and lasting solutions (meaning: God-centered solutions).

Among the first things we will notice is just how far removed we are from the "noble, strong America" that has been painted as the necessary tool to justify the never-ending expansion of the progressive American Empire. And this expansion, with the Everest-esque mountains of debt that it has inspired, has been most boldly advocated by the "conservative" wing of the American Progressive movement: The contemporary American Republican Party.

It is interesting to consider recent and present American Republican leadership in light of biblical warnings regarding false prophets.

The constant promise of freedom or the defense of freedom or advancing the cause of freedom...these are familiar devices. They are tried and true tools of the enemy; tried and true tools of the modern progressive movement.

Consider the following warning from the Lord regarding false prophets as recorded in 2 Peter:

Bold and willful, they do not tremble as they blaspheme the glorious ones, whereas angels, though greater in might and power, do not pronounce a blasphemous judgment against them before the Lord. But these, like irrational animals, creatures of instinct, born to be caught and destroyed, blaspheming about matters of which they are ignorant, will also be destroyed in their destruction, suffering wrong as the wage for their wrongdoing. They count it pleasure to revel in the daytime. They are blots and blemishes, reveling in their deceptions, while they feast with you. They have eyes full of adultery, insatiable for sin. They entice unsteady souls. They have hearts trained in greed. Accursed children! Forsaking the right way, they have gone astray. They have followed the way of Balaam, the son of Beor, who loved gain from wrongdoing, but was rebuked for his own transgression; a speechless donkey spoke with human voice and restrained the prophet's madness.

These are waterless springs and mists driven by a storm. For them the gloom of utter darkness has been reserved. For, speaking loud boasts of folly, they entice by sensual passions of the flesh those who are barely escaping from those who live in error. They promise them freedom, but they themselves are slaves of corruption. For whatever overcomes a person, to that he is enslaved. For if, after they have escaped the defilements of the world through the knowledge of our Lord and Savior Jesus Christ, they are again entangled in them and overcome, the last state has become worse for them than the first. For it would have been better for them never to have known the way of righteousness than after knowing it to turn back from the holy commandment delivered to them. What the true proverb says has happened to them: "The dog returns to its own vomit, and the sow, after washing herself, returns to wallow in the mire." (2 Peter 2:10-22)

Every God-hating, man-centered impulse of every non-Christian component of this fading world will recoil and retaliate against any move that we might make or encourage to consider such issues as these in such a light as this. Yet we can do no other.

We must see just what the ideals of this "empire of ideals" are founded upon and, where we find the man-centered, secularly pragmatic standards of the world holding sway, we must "tear down enemy strongholds" and advance the cause of Christ's glory and Kingdom by the means with which He has graced us as modern day American Christians. The neo-conservative/progressive policies of perpetual war and domestic servitude to the war machine can no longer be allowed the cover or support of those of us who proclaim Christ as Lord over all.

Does this make us pacifists? No. Does this mean that we reject the notion of a "just war"? No. Not at all, though these are some of the reflexive, suppressive tags that will be immediately hurled our way whenever we dare even raise these sorts of questions.

A God-glorifying America is possible. A God-glorifying American military is possible. The worldwide influence of such a force would be a wonderful thing....but this is not where we are. More precisely, this is not where we have been led...intentionally and progressively led...

This American Empire is built upon the foundation of sand that Jesus described in Matthew 7. It needs a foundation of rock in order to survive. Without it, this empire is doomed to fail and fall as all other self-serving, man-exalting empires have before it. This situation requires a supernatural foundation transformation.

By the grace of God, that is exactly what we have been given. The lost American nation can be found in Him, one individual at a time, through the only tool by which He has promised to save men: His perfect, supernatural Gospel.

As we proclaim that God is holy, man is evil, judgment is coming, that Christ has lived the perfect life and died as the perfect sacrifice so that those who believe upon Him will be saved and spared the coming judgment, this nation - including its military ad military policies - can, if it is God's will, be transformed, one soldier and one marine and one pilot and one nurse and one Senator and one President at a time. As we dutifully, humbly, but firmly proclaim the Gospel command to repent, believe, and be saved, Americans will, by His grace, repent, believe, and be saved. And then they will seek His will. Then they will ask questions, and seek answers according to that new, supernaturally imposed appetite for Him as the truth upon which they are compelled to feed.

These supernaturally reborn Americans will then slip off the shackles of wrong ideas, including the stupid neo-con trick we have discussed here, and its closely related cousin, which will be the subject of the next chapter: The Stupid Worship America Trick.

THE AMERICA IDOL

THE STUPID WORSHIP AMERICA TRICK

God bless America,
Land that I love.
Stand beside her, and guide her
Through the night with a light from above.

GOD BLESS
AMERICA

"I believe we are on an irreversible trend toward more freedom and democracy - but that could change."

DAN QUAYLE

"War is peace. Freedom is slavery. Ignorance is strength."

GEORGE ORWELL, *1984*

The closest thing that the enemy has to a superweapon in the battle for American political will is blind faith in the American system and state. Blind, stupid faith - a faith made possible only through a lifetime of ignorance-fueled indoctrination prepared, promoted, and reinforced by the very system and state in question. The typical American citizen's programmed, perverted notion of the system's untested and unexplored invincibility is the feeble, broken down, rusted out little lynch pin holding the whole rotten machine together.

America's imminent collapse is an unthinkable thought to the mind of the thoroughly programmed and dependent drone, and such drone status now sadly defines the vast majority of the nation's population.

The thought that any Christian is currently captivated by this profoundly warped view of American invincibility is one that should all the more motivate our pursuit of truth in political and social realms through conversations aimed at understanding and exalting the will of God in all places. As nearly every American brother and sister in Christ is struggling to one extent or another to free themselves, by His grace, from the fog of America and Americanism worship that defines so much of the political discourse in the nation - particularly on the right, we must be mindful of and patient with those who are still operating under the mass of false assumptions and delusions that define the attitude of America idolization.

We are also wise to note and hold close the truth that apart from the supernaturally salvific work of the Gospel of Christ in the life of one who is lost, they cannot see, much less understand, much less choose, the truth of God.

As all who are unsaved and remain unrepentant before the Lord are literally enslaved to their spiritually dead natures, we should aim first and always to guide them toward the Gospel of Christ. Only after they have been saved by His grace through His Gospel can we have any real hope of bringing them to embrace His will in any other area of life, and doubly so when it comes to the worldview permeating American idolatry that defines the typical secular (and many a professing Christian) American mind.

Explaining to such folks why it is that they should set aside their idolization of the nation, or any other idol, for that matter, is pure silliness (and a huge waste of time and breath) when we know full well that, biblically speaking, they can do nothing *but* worship one false idol or another in their present state of self-obsessed, self-serving, and self-referential spiritual blindness and death. They need the Gospel. Only the Gospel can open their eyes, minds, and hearts to the truth. Only the Gospel can propel God to the pinnacle of concern in their lives and displace any warped views of American idolatry that have usurped His rightful position as the only worthy object of undivided adoration and glory.

Until and unless this supernatural salvation happens in the life of a sinner, they are bound to go right on sincerely, obliviously singing "God Bless America" while supporting a government and system wholly at war with the God in question.

Until and unless a miraculous, divine intervention raises the spiritually dead to life through the Gospel proclamation, that dead man or woman will continue to imagine that the material plunder and comfort that has been granted them by way of the coasting-toward-oblivion American economic system will continue to cushion their life forever and ever and ever. Things like math and sustainability do not matter to them. Such realities simply do not register, because they cannot be allowed to do so. The bubble world of the welfare state dependent slave cannot suffer even the thought of such pinpricks.

For the sake of this new, state system-fueled "America worship", Americans have, en masse, surrendered liberty after liberty, sacrificed the future economic survival, much less prosperity, of their children, and, most importantly, formally abandoned any distinct reliance upon truth and its Author as the basis upon which anything of consequence is done in the nation. And each of these progressions away from God's perfect truth and towards man-centered pseudo-realities have been vigorously promoted and advanced by the leadership of the contemporary American Republican party.

In the modern era of perpetual invasion and occupation, "we have always been at war with Eastasia". In the modern era of George W. Bush having "abandoned free market principles to save the free market system" and the normalization of TSA molestation for the sake of our protection, "freedom has become slavery". And in the new normal of mass-produced, properly programmed, pro-state drones, "ignorance has become strength".

It is 1984.

And it will remain 1984 until and unless God graces us with the one and only thing that can save us from this increasingly Orwellian nightmare: A Christ-centered reformation, revival, and revolution.

America is not *the* answer. Conservatism is not *the* answer. Free markets and capitalism are not *the* answers. The Gospel of Jesus Christ is the one, only, and first essential answer, and all of these other things, wonderful though they may be when they are explicitly defined and pursued according to His will, are incapable of inching this nation or culture or even one single solitary individual man or woman one single inch into a true and lasting place of peace and prosperity.

Where once America - along with its political conservatism and Republicanism to a significant extent - was associated with the God-centeredness so precious and essential to a Christian worldview and life in practice, the modern conservative movement and Republican Party establishment has built its castle on a foundation of sand, and the storms are coming to blow that house down even as this is being written.

While there are many faces and man-centered foundation points to the secular, self-serving conservatism that has come to shape the majority view within the Republican Party, there is one fairly recent face and philosophy that offers us a good glimpse into the ugly truth of much of what passes itself off as modern conservatism and libertarianism. This relatively fresh reference point is found in the philosophy and worldview of Ayn Rand.

OBJECTIVELY CHRISTLESS

"This is my commandment, that you love one another as I have loved you. **Greater love has no one than this, that someone lay down his life for his friends.** *You are my friends if you do what I command you."*

JESUS (THE REAL ONE) IN JOHN 15:12-14
(BOLD EMPHASIS ADDED)

"I swear, by my life and my love of it, that I will never live for the sake of another man, nor ask another man to live for mine."

AYN RAND, *ATLAS SHRUGGED*

Ayn Rand (1905-1982) was the author of two best-selling, influential novels, *Atlas Shrugged*, and *The Fountainhead*, and the founder of a philosophical system that she dubbed "Objectivism". Her books and the ideas contained therein are wildly popular among those with conservative and libertarian political inclinations. Her slogans can be seen on signs at Tea Party events and her thoughts have been praised by Rush Limbaugh. Ayn Rand is a big deal on the conservative and libertarian political scenes.

As an atheist, she denied God and the supernatural. As a political philosopher, she advocated an explicitly self-centered, self-serving approach to pretty much everything; a "rugged individualism" the likes of which has natural appeal to the secular conservative and libertarian. Her views couldn't be more clearly anti-Christian, yet they do harmonize well with much of the modern conservative movement in America.

OBJECTIVELY DOOMED

"The purpose of morality is to teach you, not to suffer and die, but to enjoy yourself and live."

AYN RAND

Whoever seeks to preserve his life will lose it, but whoever loses his life will keep it.

LUKE 17:33

The self-serving, self-centered, materialistic, hedonistic core of such secularly inspired and inspiring philosophies as Rand's Objectivism are hard to miss as being largely representative of modern secular thought - be it conservative, libertarian, or just plain *American*. We are a people committed to self-serving, materialistic pursuits. In these pursuits, we are practical objectivists almost as often as we are practical atheists.

This objectivist inclination is tailor made to fit and feed the "America Worship" mode that has come to be a primary source of sustaining the nation's slide into statism.

America - and American secular conservatism -finds itself more and more defined by and reliant upon the self-serving slogans and philosophies portrayed by Orwell in *1984* and advocated by Rand in *Atlas Shrugged*.

Perpetual spending for the sake of eventual financial stability.

Perpetual war for the sake of eventual peace.

Perpetual selfishness for the sake of a happy civilization.

"Ignorance is strength", as Orwell once wrote, and we are now reaping the fruits of our persistent aversion to truth and its Author.

We have abandoned the beautiful truths that God has given us first through theology and then in theologically driven sociology,

132

economics, ethics, and philosophy. By chasing after our self-referential tails, we have spun ourselves silly and are left dizzy on the brink of a darkness the likes of which this nation has not yet seen.

As we watch the cumulative consequences of these catastrophic philosophical constructs engulf the nation, we are witnessing the convergence of each of these stupid elephant tricks. Secular pragmatism defines the approach of the modern Republican Party. Secular libertarianism fuels the grass-roots movements within the party. Neo-conservatism has a hammerlock on the foreign policy of the party, ensuring perpetual war for the foreseeable future if it is given the power to make such choices. And the idolization of America is the battle cry of practically everyone at every level in the G.O.P camp.

Serving as the proverbial cherry on top of this most depressing of sundaes is the presumptive pending nomination of the first openly and explicitly anti-Christian candidate of any major American political party.

Somewhere, the devil is smiling at all of this "progress"...

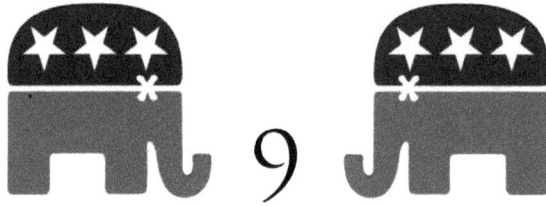

THE CHRIST-LESS
CON(VERSATION)

THE STUPID TALK ABOUT ANYTHING BUT *THE* TRUTH TRICK

Walk in wisdom toward outsiders, making the best use of the time. Let your speech always be gracious, seasoned with salt, so that you may know how you ought to answer each person.

COLOSSIANS 4:5-6

Let no corrupting talk come out of your mouths, but only such as is good for building up, as fits the occasion, that it may give grace to those who hear. And do not grieve the Holy Spirit of God, by whom you were sealed for the day of redemption.

EPHESIANS 4:29-30

One of the most simultaneously encouraging and frustrating alterations to the American cultural scene in the past few decades has been the emergence of conservative talk radio. The opportunity has been incredible, and, from a secularly pragmatic standpoint, that opportunity has been seized to great effect.

The likes of Rush Limbaugh, Sean Hannity, Laura Ingraham, Mark Levin, Alex Jones, and Glenn beck absolutely dominate the talk radio airwaves, and their corresponding presence on television has yielded similar results. Conservative and libertarian talk is wildly popular.

In many ways, this has been understandably encouraging to conservative types who, for decades prior to the emergence of "alternative" media and non-leftist media presentations, were left in something of an Orwellian media echo-chamber whose contents were almost entirely dictated by the secular leftist inclinations that permeated the "big three" on television (ABC, CBS, and NBC) and their locked-in, lock-step radio counterparts.

Progressivism, in its more liberal and leftist flavors, was the only show in town.

Then along came Rush Limbaugh and ...*vavoom!* Everything changed forever.

Rush completely changed the face - and voice and tone and content - of political speech in America and single-handedly saved the AM radio dial from its slow fade to obsolescence. Since Limbaugh paved the way and continues to lead the substantial conservative talk radio pack with the most popular show in the nation, talk radio as a whole has thrived. The most popular of programs to have come in his wake have been mostly political in nature, and of those political talk shows, virtually all of them have embraced a conservative perspective.

While there is much to be savored and celebrated in Rush's reshaping of talk in America from a purely secular political perspective, there are some significant concerns that ought not be overlooked by Christians. As we are, by nature, properly inclined in a very conservative direction on most issues, we are therefore also inclined toward particular temptations of the enemy. In our desire to see certain political perspectives or positions expressed and advanced, we can be very susceptible to Christ-less detours from the Christ-centered path we are commanded to hold and proclaim.

Sadly, that's exactly what has happened throughout the world of conservative talk radio.

RELENTLESS AVOIDANCE OF THE TRUTH

"All must admit that the reception of the teachings of Christ results in the purest patriotism, in the most scrupulous fidelity to public trust, and in the best type of citizenship."

GROVER CLEVELAND

But you are a chosen race, a royal priesthood, a holy nation, a people for his own possession, that you may proclaim the excellencies of him who called you out of darkness into his marvelous light.

1 PETER 2:9

As I mentioned earlier, I was once a pretty big Rush fan. And as I happily report now, I still am. But when I hear or remember Rush's oh-so-oft-repeated introductory tagline regarding his professed "relentless pursuit of the truth", and I test this "pursuit" in light of the pure Truth of Scripture, I am...well...bummed - both bummed for Rush and bummed for his audience.

While claiming this "relentless pursuit of truth" for three hours a day and five days a week over the course of decades now, the Rush Limbaugh Show has neither examined nor expounded upon so much as a thimble full of deep, theological truth. Any way we slice it, that is pathetic.

That he or we would ever imagine for even a moment that such an approach to truth's "relentless pursuit" could ultimately produce anything truly good and positively transformative for the American culture is another fine (meaning: real and sad) example of our secular pragmatism completely trumping our biblical understanding of what (and Who) truth is, and how this truth is to be rightly pursued.

In considering and critiquing any of these hosts or their fans, we must always season our words with grace - a grace fueled by the realization that we all have only the insight and inclination that He has given us. In knowing and embracing this truth, we can firmly but respectfully encourage one another to seek God not as a vaguely defined occasional accessory to our political thought and commentary, but as the central and guiding Light of it all, and we can do so with a proper Spirit of personal humility.

By the grace of God, we can "relentlessly pursue the truth." Moreover, and also by His grace, we who He has bought with a price and equipped for the mission at hand, are able and commanded to do just that: Relentlessly pursue the truth.

The real truth.

The whole truth.

The literal embodiment of truth: The living Lord Jesus Christ.

This is where our political theory and thought ought to gravitate, and explicitly so. And this is precisely where the largest contemporary conservative political talk shows will not go...for now. But that can change and, Lord willing, it will. Where the present conservative political talk universe is dominated by the same secular standards that motivate the rest of the culture, it need not remain that way. When we submit to Him all things, and we exercise the freedom of speech that He has lovingly provided Christian Americans while it is still in hand, we can bring a genuine relentless pursuit of Truth and its Author to the airwaves.

As long as we yield to the temptation to "pursue truth" in such a Christ-less, Scripture-free manner as that which currently defines most of "our" political talk, we are, quite simply, doomed. A

PURSUING THE PURSUIT OF TRUTH

Brothers, join in imitating me, and keep your eyes on those who walk according to the example you have in us. For many, of whom I have often told you and now tell you even with tears, walk as enemies of the cross of Christ. Their end is destruction, their god is their belly, and they glory in their shame, with minds set on earthly things. But **our citizenship is in heaven, and from it we await a Savior, the Lord Jesus Christ**

PHILIPPIANS 3:17-20

We cannot settle for America worship or freedom worship or liberty worship or capitalism worship or free market worship. We must only accept, and will only thrive, through explicitly God-focused worship, and that explicit identification of the one true God as the one and only true source of any genuinely good and lasting thing must be the central, guiding principle of our political speech and the pursuit of any political truth.

We cannot "save America" by any other means because we cannot please God by any other approach. He has spoken plainly. All we need to is obey. And when our favorite talk radio shows don't seem all that interested in that particular sort of "relentless pursuit of the truth", we should pray that God might change them, and then do whatever He positions and equips us to do to help them along the way.

SECTION FOUR

~

Godless Old Party Leadership

10

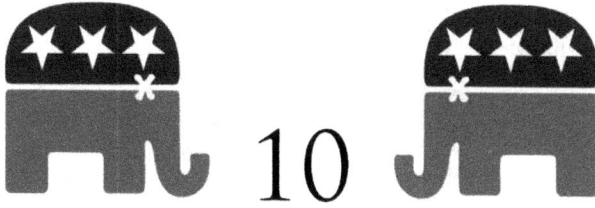

THE WOULD BE GOD WHO WOULD BE PRESIDENT

THE BEAUTY (GREAT HAIR) AND HORROR (WRONG GOD) OF EXPLICITLY UNBIBLICAL LEADERSHIP

> *...what partnership has righteousness with lawlessness? Or what fellowship has light with darkness? What accord has Christ with Belial? Or what portion does a believer share with an unbeliever? What agreement has the temple of God with idols? For we are the temple of the living God...*
>
> 2 CORINTHIANS 6:14-16

"Of two evils, choose neither."

CHARLES HADDON SPURGEON

"Oh yeah, I know *all* about it. It's incredible! Truly an *amazing* thing! If you work hard enough and you are a good enough guy here and now in the eyes of the god of this world – who, by the way, was once just a fallen man like you – he will then, in turn, make you the god of your own little planet. Wow! What's not to like about that?"

The nicely dressed young man's eyes widened a bit at this unusual response to his question.

"And after he green lights you for that supercool promotion, you get these *amazing* perks, including all the eternal sex you can handle with your multiple(!) totally-devoted-to-your-needs spirit wives. Quite naturally, the offspring from those never-ending celestial happy times will then go on to become the souls of the people populating the little planet over which you are god."

By the time the subject of eternal celestial polygamous sex came along, the increasingly concerned young questioner-turned-listener had completely lost track of the warm smile that had accompanied his asking of the initial question in the first place.

"Then, of course, those people born under *your* godship, if they are wise enough, work hard enough, and are good enough in *your* eyes, can themselves earn a shot onto the same supercool track to god-ness; an eternity long path with no beginning and no end – just an unbroken, unending line of men becoming gods and women becoming eternal soul/baby-makers stretching as far into the past and future as anyone can see or imagine. Yeah, that makes perfect sense."

By now passers-by at the Battlefield Mall were starting to slow down and pay attention. It didn't help that the response, however kindly it was being made, was also being spoken with a precision and at a volume that sure seemed aimed, at least in part, at those increasingly interested bystanders.

"No true beginning. No end in sight. Just innumerable men-made-gods living out the most polytheistic religion imaginable, each going about their eternities enjoying a whole lotta power and, of course, a whole lotta sex with a whoooooooole lotta women. Neato! Whatta deal, huh!? Well, maybe not so much if you're a woman, but that's obviously beside the point. This has to be a pretty easy sell for guys at least, right? I mean, guys who like sex and power, anyway. And since you apparently would like all of the power, all of the sex, and all of the sex partners that come as a part of that rather amazing sounding godhood package, you are here at the mall talking with me today. That's pretty much it, right?"

This was not how or where the conversation was supposed to go. This was not the answer that the young man was looking for when he so politely and kindly escorted his simple, sincere question to its target with the warmest of smiles and a friendly, firm hand shake. And before the young man could respond, it got worse.

"I do appreciate that the name 'Jesus' was included in your question, since the single most important question that any of us can ask or consider is, 'Who is Jesus?'"

Aha! *Jesus!* Now there was a term – a name, *the* name – that would surely unite all parties involved in the conversation...or maybe not...

"Of course, the name 'Jesus' is only as good or bad as the person to whom it is attached, so we can probably both agree that it's always important to be sure that we're talking about the same *person* when we use the same name. I mean, a lot of very different people can go by the same name."

AN ANTICHRIST BY ANY OTHER NAME...

I am astonished that you are so quickly deserting him who called you in the grace of Christ and are turning to a different gospel— not that there is another one, but there are some who trouble you and want to distort the gospel of Christ. But even if we or an angel from heaven should preach to you a gospel contrary to the one we preached to you, let him be accursed. As we have said before, so now I say again: If anyone is preaching to you a gospel contrary to the one you received, let him be accursed.

GALATIANS 1:6-8

But I am afraid that as the serpent deceived Eve by his cunning, your thoughts will be led astray from a sincere and pure devotion to Christ. For if someone comes and proclaims another Jesus than the one we proclaimed, or if you receive a different spirit from the one you received, or if you accept a different gospel from the one you accepted, you put up with it readily enough.

2 CORINTHIANS 11: 3,4

For false christs and false prophets will arise and perform great signs and wonders, so as to lead astray, if possible, even the elect.

MATTHEW 24:24

"Think of it this way: If I had kids and was in urgent need of a baby-sitter one day, and I'd heard from the most reliable of sources that a wonderful woman named Barbara was hands-down the most amazing babysitter ever to grace the face of the planet, and that she would very much like to watch over *my* children, I wouldn't just run up to the first woman named Barbara who presented herself as a good babysitter and hand over my kids, would I? Of course not! I'd wanna be sure that she was not only *a* Barbara, but *the* Barbara with whom my children would be most safe, secure, and well cared for – *especially* if the same "most reliable of sources" that had told me of *the* Barbara had also warned me that there would be many *other* Barbaras out there roaming the countryside seeking to fool me for the purpose of doing unimaginable harm to me and my children.

If the Bible describes Jesus as God, the infinite, pre-existent Son, and you bring to me a Jesus who is the finite, created brother of Lucifer, and most certainly *not* God, then whatever anyone might think of either of these descriptions, it should, at the very least, be apparent that we are each talking about two different Jesuses. If the Bible describes God as the transcendent, eternally holy Creator and Sustainer of all things at all times, and you bring to me a god who was once just a fallen man like you or me and had to earn his way to godhood, we are then also quite obviously talking about two very different gods. And if the Bible describes the fear and knowledge of the Lord Jesus Christ as the beginning of all true wisdom, all true knowledge, and a supernaturally salvific relationship with Him as the only way to salvation, then I am obviously compelled to stand against your false savior, your false gospel, and your false church...even if it calls itself the Church of Jesus Christ of Latter-Day Saints."

A lot has changed since the increasingly distant '90s, when I was blessed with the cool Mormon missionary encounter on that busy day at the Battlefield Mall. America has since been subjected to a variety of self-inflicted tragedies like President Bill Clinton, Lady Gaga, and Jar Jar Binks, and while it's debatable as to which has been most damaging to the culture, there is little doubt that one question haunts this land far more than even the likes of Bubba and Jar Jar.

The question is as simple and profound as it was when Christ first asked it: "Who do *you* say that I am?"

The answer to this question is *everything*...no matter how much the enemy and his drones would have us to believe otherwise. It really does radically influence our understanding of everything in His creation – every object, idea, concept and dream. The greatest of things, the smallest of things, and everything in between – they are all fundamentally shaped by our understanding of who He is.

So it is that we shouldn't be surprised that every stupid elephant trick under consideration has only been made useful to the enemy by way of our ignorance of and/or disinterest in the nature of the one true God. And it should be even less surprising that a political party so thoroughly disinterested in that God would find itself proudly perched on the precipice of becoming the first majot American political party to nominate an explicitly anti-Christian man to become the next President of the United States of America.

Even Barack Obama had to at least fake some form of vaguely pseudo-orthodox Christianity...but not the G.O.P nominee...not anymore...

THE CONSERVATIVE DEFENSE OF CHRISTLESSNESS

"The Mormon religion takes care of their own. They don't have people on welfare...they believe in a greater being."

Former First Lady Barbara Bush, defending
Mitt Romney's religion on *Larry King Live*

Have nothing to do with the fruitless deeds of darkness, but rather expose them.

Ephesians 5:11

We have much to thank God for here. The real one, I mean.

In Mitt Romney's ascendance, the Lord has given each and every one of us who have a voice in the American political system and claim Christ as Lord a wonderful opportunity. We have the opportunity to define and defend the depth and detail of His character and nature as He has so clearly revealed it in His perfect Word. For this, we should all give thanks in prayer...and then we should act.

And again, the particular portion of the action advocated in these pages is but one step down a long, important path: The serious, biblical contemplation of political questions. And candidates.

What is Mormonism, anyway? Is it Christian? Does it matter? Is it important to know a candidate's understanding of the nature of God? Is the "fear of the Lord" *really* the beginning of wisdom and the beginning of knowledge, as the Bible repeatedly says? If it is, isn't it very important that we, as obedient Christians, choose a leader who worships the right and real Lord so that he might actually have that entry level, "beginning of" true knowledge and true wisdom?

These are important questions. We cannot allow the opportunity to stand for truth and its Author through the serious pursuit of these questions to slip through fingers by yielding to the temptation to follow the Grand Old Party line , which will center on one of the following approaches:

A. Dismiss the question out of hand and make anyone asking feel silly for doing so.

B. Pretend that Mormonism is Christian simply because its adherents claim that it is so, and make anyone interested in testing that claim feel silly for doing so.

C. Attack anyone who persists in these questions by painting them as intolerant bigots and/or fanatical religious zealot nutcases.

In other words, progressive Republicans will do *exactly* what progressive Democrats do when faced with such questions. That oughta tell us something, and when it happens we should be anything but surprised.

The Bushes love Romney. Karl Rove loves Romney. Bob Dole and John McCain support Romney. Even the beloved Ann Coulter is all about some Mitt in 2012.

And you should support Romney, too!

I mean, you don't want Obama to win, now do you?

A MOST DANGEROUS ENEMY

"A nation can survive its fools, and even the ambitious. But it cannot survive treason from within. An enemy at the gates is less formidable, for he is known and carries his banner openly. But the traitor moves amongst those within the gate freely, his sly whispers rustling through all the alleys, heard in the very halls of government itself. For the traitor appears not a traitor; he speaks in accents familiar to his victims, and he wears their face and their arguments, he appeals to the baseness that lies deep in the hearts of all men. He rots the soul of a nation, he works secretly and unknown in the night to undermine the pillars of the city, he infects the body politic so that it can no longer resist. A murderer is less to fear. The traitor is the plague."

MARCUS TULLIUS CICERO

You've probably heard many folks recite something along the lines of, "I'd vote for the Devil himself before I'd vote for [insert hated alternative to Devil here]." And sadly, that's quite close to what they end up doing most of the time in such scenarios. When the "lesser of two evils" is chosen, evil wins elections. And Cthulhu smiles.

When the "lesser evil" is championed by professing followers of the Lord Jesus Christ, we are truly in a bad place and on the verge of much, much worse. With the prospective presidential nomination of Mitt Romney by the Republican Party, we are in just such a place and perfectly positioned for just such a fall.

THE SATANIC IMPULSE

"How you are fallen from heaven,
  O Day Star, son of Dawn!
How you are cut down to the ground,
  you who laid the nations low!
You said in your heart,
  'I will ascend to heaven;
above the stars of God
  I will set my throne on high;
I will sit on the mount of assembly
  in the far reaches of the north;
I will ascend above the heights of the clouds;
  I will make myself like the Most High.'"

ISAIAH 14:12-14

"As man is, God once was; as God is, man may become."

LDS PRESIDENT LORENZO SNOW

"There are some [who would] would prefer it if I would simply distance myself from my religion, say that it's more of a tradition than my personal conviction, or disavow one or another of its precepts. That I will not do. I believe in my Mormon faith and I endeavor to live by it."

MITT ROMNEY

This is not intended to be a deep study of Mormonism. Such a study is unnecessary. The truth required here for our purposes is quick to surface and easy to identify for any with ears to hear, eyes to see, and a heart that is desirous of pursuing truth wherever it leads. When the first and most essential question is answered as boldly, as clearly, and in as explicitly an anti-Christian manner as the Mormon religion has provided, we can know, quickly and certainly, that the group is openly opposed to biblical Christianity.

That first and most essential question is, of course: Who is God?

Or, put another way, by God the Son, *"Who do you say that I am?"*

This is the question of questions, and the Mormon answer to this question harmonizes perfectly with the original satanic impulse, as is evidenced in the following sentiments embraced and exalted as truth by the Mormon religion:

> "We have imagined and supposed that God was God from all eternity. I will refute that idea, and take away the veil, so that you may see."
>
> *TEACHINGS OF THE PROPHET JOSEPH SMITH,* PP.345

> "God himself was once as we are now, and is an exalted Man, and sits enthroned in yonder heavens...I say, if you were to see him to-day, you would see him like a man in form -- like yourselves, in all the person, image, and very form as a man....it is necessary that we should understand the character and being of God, and how he came to be so; for I am going to tell you how God came to be God. We have imagined and supposed that God was God from all eternity, I will refute that idea, and will take away and do away the veil, so that you may see....and that he was once a man like us; yea, that God himself the Father of us all, dwelt on an earth the same as Jesus Christ himself did."
>
> *JOURNAL OF DISCOURSES,* VOL. 6, P. 3

"In the beginning, the head of the Gods called a council of the Gods; and they came together and concocted a plan to create the world and people it,"

JOURNAL OF DISCOURSES,
VOL. 6, P. 5

In its exaltation of man to the place of God, Mormonism's core satanic impulse is clear for all to see...and we must not pretend otherwise, no matter how secularly pragmatic such aversion to critical truth is proclaimed to be by the culture at large.

Christianity is, at its core, *essentially* monotheistic. There is *one* God. There has never been and will never be another. Judaism shares this core belief. Even Islam is monotheistic. But Mormonism? Anything but.

Mormonism is literally the most polytheistic religion in the world. It embraces a belief in a line of past man-made-into-gods that stretches backward into infinity.

In keeping with this most bizarre and unbiblical of constructs, *Mormonism has no origin account in the ultimate sense.* So it is that from the very start of Genesis' "In the beginning" account, Mormonism departs and opposes Christianity. That opposition persists through every core precept known to orthodox Christianity just as one would expect from any faith that so clearly denies the most basic truth about the nature of God: His exclusivity.

So if the "fear of the Lord is the beginning of wisdom" and "the beginning of knowledge", and we know that, by his own profession of faith in the infinitely polytheistic, beginning-less, endless, anti-Christian religion of Mormonism, which inherently includes his embrace of the explicitly satanic belief that he can one day be god, then what is a biblical Christian to do when it comes to Mitt Romney's pursuit of the highest, and most culturally impactful, office in the land (and even the world)?

It's okay to ask...really...

Actually, it's more than okay. It's *essential*.

NOTHING TO SEE HERE...MOVE ALONG

"Father O'Donovan asked me to speak on how faith informs my public service. **I'd never talked about my faith publicly.** I mean, I acknowledge that I'm a practicing Catholic, but I don't think it's anybody's business, nor do I think it should matter to anyone. That's why I'm so angry about the way they're treating Romney."[7]

VICE PRESIDENT JOE BIDEN
(EMPHASIS ADDED)

"I really, really like Mike Huckabee. He's a good, fine man...but **for him to come out and say, 'well, I don't know if I would vote for a Mormon or not' is really, honestly reprehensible.**

...it's not about our faith, it's about our principles. I just want to know that a man believes in something...and will actually stand up for what he believes in. **That's the way you vote for President.**"

GLENN BECK
(EMPHASIS ADDED)

Remember: Even asking this sort of question is a no-no. It's a problem, and a big one at that. You just shouldn't go there, and you won't if you know what's good for ya. And what's good for the country. Or so goes the secularly pragmatic pitch, anyway.

But if there's one thing we can hopefully agree upon at this point, it is that secular pragmatism is not the guiding philosophy of Christians...so ask this sort of question we must, and ask it we will.

---

[7] Politico, 12.14.11 - http://www.politico.com/news/stories/1211/70416.html

And while we're on the subject of questions that "they" would rather we not contemplate, much less ask, here are a few more keepers for our good and proper and God glorifying consideration:

- Can a Christian *ever* glorify God by disregarding (aka "disobeying") His revealed will?

- Can a Christian ever *expect* God-glorifying cultural leadership or change to come through a God-hating man or woman (which the Bible states is the condition of all unrepentant, unconverted mankind)?

- Should a Christian *ever* cast his or her God-given vote in support of an *explicitly* non- (or anti-) Christian candidate (not to be confused with an *imperfect* candidate, which all men are)?

- When He finally judges all of their actions, as He has promised to do, what will Jesus Christ have to say to those who spent *His* vote in support of leadership that openly denied and opposed Him?

- Can we as Christians honestly expect that our God will heal our devastated culture as we claim to desire that He would when, alongside our pleas, prayers and claims for His healing, we openly choose leadership that is at war with Him?

- If God has made plain that we must never have or worship (meaning glorify in any way) any other "god", then how might He feel about our casting a vote for a man who believes that he will become god, all so that our vote might propel this god-wannabe into a leadership position over us?

If our God is real to us, these questions will matter. We will seek His will in them. And if we love Him, we *will* keep His commandments.

156

SECTION FIVE

~

The Power of Political Repentance and Restoration

11

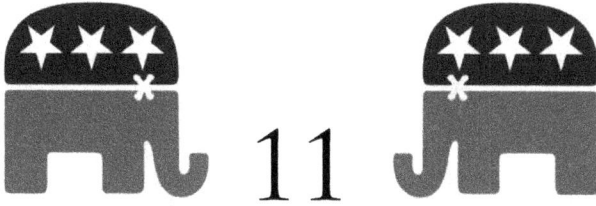

OBEDIENCE IN (POLITICAL) ACTION

THE GOSPEL RESPONSE TO STUPID ELEPHANT TRICKS

> *When Pharaoh drew near, the people of Israel lifted up their eyes, and behold, the Egyptians were marching after them, and they feared greatly. And the people of Israel cried out to the LORD. They said to Moses, "Is it because there are no graves in Egypt that you have taken us away to die in the wilderness? What have you done to us in bringing us out of Egypt? Is not this what we said to you in Egypt: 'Leave us alone that we may serve the Egyptians'? For it would have been better for us to serve the Egyptians than to die in the wilderness." And Moses said to the people, "Fear not, stand firm, and see the salvation of the LORD, which he will work for you today. For the Egyptians whom you see today, you shall never see again. The LORD will fight for you, and you have only to be silent."*

> EXODUS 14:10-14

I love *The Ten Commandments*. The movie, I mean. The actual commandments, I of course adore, but what I'm talking about here is that legendary '50s flick featuring Charlton Heston, Yul Brynner, and some of the most awe-inspiringly cheesy special effects ever made.

There are many great moments and scenes in the Cecil B. DeMille masterpiece, but probably the most iconic is the parting of the Red Sea before Moses' outstretched arms.

We know and treasure the history that inspired this moment of movie magic: God led Moses to lead the just-freed-from-bondage-to-Egypt people of Israel to the shore of the Red Sea as the armies of a hardened and angry Pharaoh rushed toward them. God's people literally were backed into an impossible, life-threatening situation...right where He wanted them.

And as they were (and are) so prone to do, God's people (and many in the crowd who were merely pretending to be God's people) lashed out angrily at the man who had led them to where God had told him to lead them. They openly repudiated him and his God, begging for the chance to go back to Egypt in bondage, rather than follow this Moses and his God to death.

These were, and are, very *pragmatic* people. Everything that their eyes told them screamed "this is a bad place to be". Everything that their minds absorbed about the situation shouted "we are fools for standing *here* with *him*". And everything in their self-serving, self-referential, self-preservation obsessed little hearts said, "surely it is better to live in bondage to Egypt than to follow this man and his God to our deaths here in the desert."

In a nutshell, the trouble with man-centered pragmatism is that it's silly, dumb, and lethal. Always. It is the sort of stupid thing that can literally be led from a lifelong slavery in the most dramatic, emphatic manner imaginable, then be guided through the desert by a pillar of smoke by day and a pillar of fire by night, and then, when faced with the next obvious place for a miracle on a path literally swimming with supernatural, miraculous delivery after supernatural, miraculous delivery, it leads its people to say: This is dumb! It just can't work. I mean, what are we doing even considering allowing ourselves to be drawn into such a place by such a God as this?

And then, by His grace and in spite of the incalculable idiocy and disrespect of the people He is saving, He saves them anyway. Perfectly. Again.

BE STILL AND KNOW THAT <u>HE IS GOD</u>

The LORD said to Moses, "Why do you cry to me? Tell the people of Israel to go forward. Lift up your staff, and stretch out your hand over the sea and divide it, that the people of Israel may go through the sea on dry ground. And I will harden the hearts of the Egyptians so that they shall go in after them, and I will get glory over Pharaoh and all his host, his chariots, and his horsemen. And the Egyptians shall know that I am the LORD, when I have gotten glory over Pharaoh, his chariots, and his horsemen."

EXODUS 14:15-18

This actually happened, which is no doubt the tip top reason why the '56 film, with all of its corny moments and cheesy effects, moves me deeply. Just watching those people in that place with that attitude and then seeing God do what He had always planned and was always going to do in that place, in that moment, and for those people - and *perfectly* so, I cannot help but get a chill.

That is our God! That's what He does!

When we consider this Exodus example and the scores of other examples that permeate Scripture, we are left with a handful of inescapable conclusions, including:

1. Questioning God's wisdom is ultimately stupid.

2. Obeying God's direction is ultimately rewarding.

    ...and...

3. Warring against God's people is ultimately futile.

These three truths of Scripture and history as God has so lovingly recorded them for our benefit and His glory, would seem to make quite a compelling argument against just the sort of man-centered pragmatism that drives modern American Christianity in general and Christian conservative political thought in general.

And what does this make of our witness? What does this tell the world about our *actual* faith?

Is our faith in ourselves or is it in God? And make no mistake, it cannot be in both - if we are trusting first and foremost in our judgment, our wisdom, and our good pragmatic standards, then we are at least as dumb and twice as silly as the mob of pragmatic pseudo-believers that Moses had to drag through the desert.

God doesn't need you. He doesn't need me. And He doesn't need America. But make no mistake, He will use each of the three to accomplish His will according to His purposes, and perfectly so.

As we see in Romans 1, our nation has already fallen under the judgment of God. This is undeniable. He has "given us over" to ourselves, and the end is near.

The enemies of God and His people are emboldened as never before. Even now, they race for what they see as the quick, final kill in their quest to remove all vestiges of the God they hate from *their* culture - the progressive, man-centered utopian dream that is finally within their grasp. The faux believers from within the Christian camp openly question God, His Word, and everything linked to either of them with a venom and persistence that betrays their true allegiance. And the culture at large, almost completely defined by these enemies from within and without the professing Christian realm, stands and cheers the fast approaching chariots, anxious for the day that these Christians and their God and His word and His rules and Hus truth might finally be wiped away completely and forever.

In the midst of this perfect storm of secularism and man-centered, God-hating *progress*, the people of God look, wonder, and...*obey*.

By His grace and for His glory, they obey.

They stand.

And He delivers.

OUR STAND - HIS GLORY

. . . Behold, to obey is better than sacrifice. . .

1 SAMUEL 15:22

"We Recognize no Sovereign but God, and no King but Jesus!"

JOHN HANCOCK AND JOHN ADAMS

What if God really *is* God?

What if He has deliberately, purposefully placed you and me right here and right now? What if He has chosen to place us in a nation that has been uniquely blessed by Him, has long since abandoned Him, and now stands shouting defiantly even as His wrath descends upon its head? What if He has perfectly positioned us in a land known for gluttonous excess and murderous narcissism the likes of which the world has never seen? What if He has arranged all of these things and all of their paths so that they might providentially intersect at this point with His people - *us* - placed in the middle of it all for one simple purpose: To obey.

What if we actually obeyed our God and called out to Him in the Spirit of obedient submission that He has given us? What supernatural, miraculous deliverance might then come?

What might happen to Pharaoh's chariots *then*?

What if the Master Storyteller, as a part of His perfect drama, has placed His people here and now so that they might glorify Him through their complete faithfulness in and reliance upon Him?

What if?

Might not it be said that all of human history has been arranged by Him so that we might have this incredible opportunity to demonstrate our true faith in Him when everything in and of the world so loudly and violently urges us to do anything but?

What He will do with our obedience, I dare not say. As stated earlier, that is His business.

But obedience is our business, and if we are to find the miraculous delivery we claim to desire at His hand, it seems as though our one and only path toward that supernatural salvation must come through submission to Him. Clearly, this opportunity will pass, and soon...

We are well served to pause here again for a moment to let the reality of our present situation soak in...

America has already fallen under the judgment of God.

Even now we are watching and experiencing it unfold around us, and soon - very soon - the enveloping wrath of a holy Sovereign will make itself plain.

To imagine that this is anything other than a most critical moment in this nation's history is to lay claim to the deepest of delusions. The hour is so late, the situation is so bleak, and the pulse is so weak that any graced with an ounce of true discernment know that we have already passed the point of no return and that nothing short of divine, supernatural intervention can save this nation.

When we see what we have freely chosen to become, we must wonder what He is about to do; from where His wrath will fall next. But as we rightly wonder and tremble at the prospect of His pure, looming judgment, we must seize the moment that He has given us. *We must seize this most precious opportunity to **repent**.*

Only through the Spirit of true and complete repentance can we be brought to Him, and only through Him can we be saved.

TIME IS SHORT...THE HOUR IS LATE... AND OUR GOD *IS* GOD

O LORD, how long shall I cry for help, and you will not hear? Or cry to you "Violence!" and you will not save? Why do you make me see iniquity, and why do you idly look at wrong? Destruction and violence are before me; strife and contention arise. So the law is paralyzed, and justice never goes forth. For the wicked surround the righteous; so justice goes forth perverted. "Look among the nations, and see; wonder and be astounded. For I am doing a work in your days that you would not believe if told. For behold, I am raising up the Chaldeans, that bitter and hasty nation, who march through the breadth of the earth, to seize dwellings not their own."

HABAKKUK 1:2-6

As God has "given over" America to her selfish desires, He is also raising up enemies from afar. As those dark clouds move our way, we have been blessed with a final, fleeting opportunity to secure the home front before the hurricane hits.

While we are still allowed to ask questions, we must. Questions of significance. Questions aimed at seeking, finding, and applying the will of God. Questions like those posed in *A Defence of Liberty Against Tyrants*. We should consider these things prayerfully:

1. Are Subjects required or even obligated to obey Princes if they command that which is against the Law of God?

2. Is it lawful to resist a Prince who actively (or only passively) resist's God's Word and His Church?

165

3. Is it lawful to resist a Prince who actively (or only passively) works to destroy the civil order and to what extent may the resistance be made?

4. Are Princes permitted or required by God's Law to give aid to the subjects of another Prince, if those people are afflicted because of their Christian faith or oppressed by obvious tyranny?

These are the questions that colonial American Christians asked. These are the questions that they took to Scripture. And these are the questions that they answered...with revolution.

As such, these are the sorts of questions that The American Progressive System simply cannot abide, so ask them we must...early, often, and as a bridge to action.

To these questions we might rightly add many pertinent inquiries, including the question of: When, and how, do we fight tyranny when it arises?

Remember, the questions alone are only as beneficial as their answers are illuminated and defined by the perfect light of Scripture. This was the Spirit of 1776. This is the answer to *1984*.

THE GOSPEL FUEL FOR THE SALVATION OF MEN, WOMEN, AND AMERICA

Where is the one who is wise? Where is the scribe? Where is the debater of this age? Has not God made foolish the wisdom of the world? For since, in the wisdom of God, the world did not know God through wisdom, it pleased God through the folly of what we preach to save those who believe. For Jews demand signs and Greeks seek wisdom, but we preach Christ crucified, a stumbling block to Jews and folly to Gentiles, but to those who are called, both Jews and Greeks, Christ the power of God and the wisdom of God. For the foolishness of God is wiser than men, and the weakness of God is stronger than men.

1 CORINTHIANS 1:20-25

But I am afraid that as the serpent deceived Eve by his cunning, your thoughts will be led astray from a sincere and pure devotion to Christ. For if someone comes and proclaims another Jesus than the one we proclaimed, or if you receive a different spirit from the one you received, or if you accept a different gospel from the one you accepted, you put up with it readily enough.

2 CORINTHIANS 11:3-4

Grace to you and peace from God our Father and the Lord Jesus Christ, who gave himself for our sins to deliver us from the present evil age, according to the

167

will of our God and Father, to whom be the glory forever and ever. Amen.

I am astonished that you are so quickly deserting him who called you in the grace of Christ and are turning to a different gospel—not that there is another one, but there are some who trouble you and want to distort the gospel of Christ. But even if we or an angel from heaven should preach to you a gospel contrary to the one we preached to you, let him be accursed.

GALATIANS 1:3-8

While we're about the business of asking all of these provocative, invigorating, and even revolutionary questions, we must never let these important pursuits distract us from the *most* incredible mission we've been given: The opportunity to boldly proclaim the Gospel of Jesus Christ, so that the questions we ask might be edifying and the scripturally sound answers we find might be cherished obeyed by those given the provided eyes to see, ears to hear, and hearts to desire and understand truth and its Author.

God is holy. Man is evil. And the judgment of a holy God against all evil is soon coming. It is into this situation that God the Father intervened, sending God the Son, Jesus, to live the perfect life that we never could so that the infinite debt owed an infinite God might be paid as it otherwise could not. God the Spirit has opened the ears, eyes, and hearts of previously dead, unbelieving men and women so that they will, when they hear His Gospel, respond with brokenness over sin, repentance, and belief. In this, they are saved by God's grace, for God's glory, and from God's wrath.

This is the supernaturally transformative message that we have been given and commanded to take to the lost, so that He might save from among them the remnant - the Bride of Christ, the Church, which will rule and reign in the restored, perfected creation to come. This is the future that He holds for His adopted children. And this is the future that should inspire us to great joy, comfort, and...obedience.

Conservatism can't save anybody. Ditto free markets. They cannot save anyone or anything that is separated from God.

Only the Gospel can raise the dead to life, and the spiritually living can properly see, much less appreciate, the Kingdom or its King.

Ours is a mission of personal submission to the King of kings. Ours is a nation and world filled with spiritually dead, natural born haters of that King. Ours is a hope that is entirely reliant upon Him, His truth, and His Gospel.

He is coming, and soon. And when He does, we will thank Him eternally for every instance during this fleeting mortal life in which He gave us the clarity, strength, and character to stand. And we will see with even greater clarity what a horror it was to have ever even entertained the notion of "choosing the lesser evil".

When we stand and walk and wonder and travel and explore and experience the never-ending splendor and adventure that He has crafted for His glory and our eternal benefit in the sin-less, evil free cosmos to come, we will know by sight what we who are His now know by faith.

May He grant us the clarity, strength, and character to challenge at every opportunity and in every realm the man-centered progress that has captivated our once inspired and inspiring nation. May He grant us the grace and love for one another that demonstrates His character in us as we go about this warfare. May He grant us the strength to stand for Him alone, by His grace alone, and for His glory alone. Amen.

*For I delivered to you as **of first importance** what I also received: that **Christ died for our sins in accordance with the Scriptures, that he was buried, that he was raised on the third day** in accordance with the Scriptures*

1 CORINTHIANS 15:3-4

FOR THE LOVE OF LINCOLN
...AND HATRED OF CTHULHU

AFTERTHOUGHTS ON CULTURE WAR AND POLITICAL REPENTANCE

"When I left Springfield I asked the people to pray for me. I was not a Christian. When I buried my son, the severest trial of my life, I was not a Christian. But when I went to Gettysburg and saw the graves of thousands of our soldiers, I then and there consecrated myself to Christ. Yes, I do love Jesus."

ABRAHAM LINCOLN

"The only means of establishing and perpetuating our republican forms of government is the universal education of our youth in the principles of Christianity by means of the Bible."

BENJAMIN RUSH

Isn't it cool to know that God *is* God?

Yeah, that was rhetorical, but it's still fun, and incredibly encouraging, to ponder. Unless your name is Cthulhu, I suppose.

Every time I even see a doubt about anything important start my way from out there on the far horizon, I always have that security in which to find perfect peace, confidence, and hope. The thought that God chose me while I still hated Him and then began the process, from my perspective anyway, of bringing me along to to complete conformity with His perfect nature so that I might one day soon explore, experience, and rule a restored creation, bringing glory to Him forever, well...I just can't really believe it. Not as I one day will believe it, anyway. Today's walk by faith will become tomorrow's walk by sight, and I am infinitely jazzed about that!

In the meantime, we have been incalculably blessed and honored. We have been raised from the dead, given supernatural life and the truth-seeking eyes, ears, and hearts that come with it. And we have been given these things in such an incredible moment in God's unfolding history that it's hard not to feel as though the imagined likes of Aragorn, Luke Skywalker, and Spider-man would, if they were real and given the chance, find themselves increasingly jealous of us with every moment spent marveling at the sheer scope and majesty of the mission to which we've been called and for which we've been perfectly equipped and positioned. Our truth is infinitely more incredible than their fiction.

Our love of the tiniest glimpses of goodness that we see when we look back at America, the Republican Party, or those who've led either or both, should inspire us - not to go "back" to or toward them, but to take the God-centered beauties contained therein, and aim to move further toward them through our pursuit of Him.

America has displayed many splendors and obvious, unique blessings from God. She has also demonstrated great darkness in her rebellion against and flight from Him. The party of Lincoln has played a great role in both the light and dark moments, with its contribution to the present darkness having been significant. It is in this context that we are graced to pray that perhaps even the Republican Party can, like Lincoln himself, be radically saved long into its life, one converted, politically active Christian at a time.

That's our mission. That's our hope.

We have been given what can be said without the slightest exaggeration to be the most incredible adventure imaginable, and our success depends on nothing more or nothing less than our faith in action through complete submission to our perfect, all-powerful Master and Commander. And make no mistake, this is a path meant for imperfect people - we will find no spotless candidates or gatherings or movements of men on this side of eternity. What we will find, and we will *always* find, is an ever-present opportunity, often appearing as an unbroken string of distinct opportunities, to achieve complete success in any thing at any time and in any place through our loving submission to Christ.

That's the path that leads to and through salvation, all by His grace and for His glory. That's the path we must walk and proclaim to a world obsessed with our diversion - a world where things like Stupid Elephant Tricks are all the rage. While we've only scratched the surface where examples of those tricks are concerned, the universal point of each one - those covered and the countless others not mentioned here, is simple: Diversion from Christ. Insofar as these diversions and distractions have been successful, the people of America have found pain, darkness, and despair. It is to these people in this country at this time that we have been brought with the one and only supernatural message capable of saving them from the darkness that now envelopes the land.

The explicitly God-centered path is the one and only way to meaningful American restoration, and that Gospel-fueled trail is the only one we have to offer...and the only one we need.

Cthulhu and Dark Helmet and Mitt Romney are rooting for alternate routes, but let's not go there, okay?

Let's love one another and love America enough to love our Lord above all, with all our hearts, minds, bodies, and *votes*. The rest will take care of itself, all according to His purpose and on His schedule. As has been rightly said by many good men, "Duty is ours. Consequences are God's."

May the Lord bless, keep, empower and encourage every Brother and Sister in Christ.

See you soon!

The following two samples are the first and the last complete chapters from *Fire Breathing Christians*.

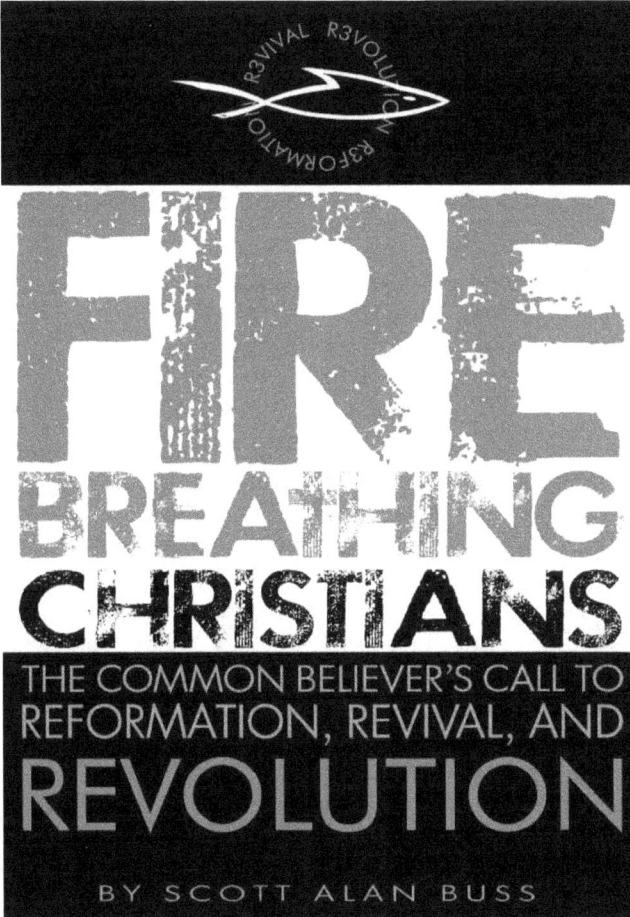

1.

WELCOME TO THE SECULAR INQUISITION

Fear and Loathing of the Common Believer

I baptize you with water for repentance, but he who is coming after me is mightier than I, whose sandals I am not worthy to carry. He will baptize you with the Holy Spirit and fire.

JOHN THE BAPTIST IN MATTHEW 3:11

And you will be hated by all for my name's sake. But the one who endures to the end will be saved.

JESUS IN MARK 13:13

"Even apart from its political implications, the rollout of the Sarah Palin vice presidential candidacy may be regarded decades from now as a nationally shared Rorschach test of enormous cultural significance." This was Jeffrey Bell's observation as recorded in *The Weekly Standard* just seventeen days after Alaska Governor Sarah Palin was selected to become Senator John McCain's running mate in the 2008 presidential campaign. He went on to describe what was rapidly becoming a perfect storm of political paranoia:

From the instant of Palin's designation on Friday, August 29, the American left went into a collective mass seizure from which it shows no sign of emerging. The left blogosphere and elite media have, for the moment, joined forces and become indistinguishable from each other, and from the supermarket tabloids, in their desire to find and use anything that will criminalize and/or humiliate Palin and her family...

In her acceptance speech last Wednesday night, anyone could see the poise and skill that undoubtedly attracted McCain's attention months ago, when few others were even aware that he was looking. But it was precisely the venom of the left's assault that heightened the drama and made it a riveting television event. Palin benefited from her ability to project full awareness of the volume and relentlessness of the attacks without showing a scintilla of resentment or self-pity.

This is a rare talent, one shared by Franklin D. Roosevelt and Ronald Reagan. For this quality to have even a chance to develop there must be something real to serve as an emotional backdrop: disproportionate, crazy-seeming rage by one's political enemies. Roosevelt was on his party's national ticket five times and Reagan sought the presidency four times. Each became governor of what at the time was the nation's most populous state. It took Roosevelt and

Reagan decades of national prominence and pitched ideological combat to achieve the gift of enemies like these. Yet the American left awarded Sarah Palin this gift seemingly within a microsecond of her appearance on the national stage in Dayton, Ohio. Why?[8]

THE ASSASSINATION OF SARAH PALIN

For the American left, reasons for fear and loathing of Sarah Palin are legion; almost too numerous to list. But we'll try anyway:

She is a woman (which would normally be a plus). She is a fiscal conservative (which offsets much of the aforementioned bonus for womanhood). She is a social conservative (this more than finishes off any remaining "female benefit"). She comes from humble roots and embraces a Judeo-Christian ethic. She is a generally happy wife and mother of five. Making matters worse on the last point, the youngest of her children, Trig, was prenatally diagnosed with Down syndrome. The problem for the secular left wasn't the diagnosis itself; it was that Mrs. Palin had subsequently allowed her son to live.

For this crime she could not be forgiven.

Little Trig became something of an unintended lightning rod as a result. The sweet little boy born to a loving, honorable Christian

---

[8] Jeffrey Bell, *Why They Hate Her* – an article published in 2008 by *The Weekly Standard* and recorded online at:
http://www.weeklystandard.com/Content/Public/Articles/000/000/015/534rly sq.asp?pg=1

mother presented to the American left a clear and present threat to the very heart of its liberal orthodoxy…by simply *living*.

With their foundations shaken and insecurities exposed, "progressive" women lashed out, leading the charge in a wild attempt to eviscerate Sarah Palin. Their seething hatred was proudly and forcefully displayed at every opportunity.

South Carolina Democrat Party chairwoman Carol Fowler pronounced that John McCain had chosen a running mate "whose primary qualification seems to be that she hasn't had an abortion." The *Washington Post*'s Wendy Doniger observed that Palin's "greatest hypocrisy is in her pretense that she is a woman." "Comedian" Margaret Cho joined the crowd of merry, blissfully content feminists by chiming in with:

"They shouldn't have the right to call themselves Christian, for they have no Christ-like attributes. I am a feminist and a Christian, and when I see Sarah Palin, I see neither. And it's official: She is evil."

Through this parade of insult and vilification, our nation was exposed to the full force and character of secular liberal womanhood. And it wasn't pretty. Then again, secular feminism rarely is or wants to be.

Eight months after Sarah Palin's acceptance speech at the Republican Party National Convention in Minneapolis-St. Paul, Minnesota, Americans were given another revealing glimpse into the philosophy shaping their nation's culture.

This moment came when a young woman from the American West committed the unpardonable sin of politically incorrect public speech. This violation of the new American speech code inspired the unrestrained wrath of vigilant thought police across the nation. The whole episode began on April 19th of 2009, when the following question echoed through the

Theatre for the Performing Arts in Planet Hollywood Resort and Casino in Las Vegas, Nevada:

> "Vermont recently became the first state to legalize same-sex marriage. Do you think every state should follow suit? Why or why not?"

This was the question asked of Carrie Prejean, representing the state of California in the Miss USA pageant. The question was asked by openly gay pageant judge Perez Hilton as a part of the Miss USA selection process.

Miss Prejean answered Hilton's politically and religiously motivated question as follows:

> "I think it's great that Americans are able to choose one or the other. We live in a land that you can choose same-sex marriage or opposite marriage. And, you know what? In my country and in my family, I think that—I believe that—a marriage should be between a man and a woman. No offense to anybody out there, but that's how I was raised and that's how I think that it should be: Between a man and a woman. Thank you."

While for many of us it may be difficult to imagine a more respectful, defensive, kind and even sheepish defense of the *actual* institution of marriage than that which Miss Prejean offered, the simple fact that she affirmed a personal belief, *when asked*, that marriage was to be "between a man and a woman," was enough for impartial, unbiased, politically, and religiously neutral judge Perez Hilton to come completely unglued.

As a result of honestly answering the question put to her in an excruciatingly polite manner consistent with the well-reasoned and time-tested beliefs of the overwhelming majority of American citizens since the founding of the nation, Carrie Prejean was denied the Miss USA crown and Perez Hilton went into full blown offended drama queen mode.

Hilton immediately recorded a video blog for release on YouTube, which included the following fabulous commentary:

"Hello...okay...so...Miss USA literally just finished and I *have* to make a video blog. Everybody's gonna be talking about it! I was *the* YouTube moment of the show—the pageant—when I asked Miss California her question, and when she gave *the...worst...answer...in pageant history!* She got *booed!* I think that was the first time in Miss USA *e-ver* that a contestant has been booed. Now, lemme explain to you: She lost, not because she doesn't believe in gay marriage. Miss California lost because she's a *dumb b----*, okay? This is how a person with half a brain answers the question I posed to her, which is: 'Vermont recently legalized same-sex marriages. Do you think other states should follow suit? Why or why not?' Well, if *I* was Miss California, with *half a brain*, I would have said, '*hmm*...Perez, that's a *great question!* That's a very *hot topic* in our country right now, and *I* think that that is a question that each state should decide for themselves, because that's how *our* forefathers designed our government, you know. The states rule themselves, and then there's certain laws which are federal.' She could have said *something* along those lines, but *she didn't!* She gave an *awful, awful* answer, which alienated *so* many people, and Miss California—Miss USA—she doesn't alienate, she *unites!* She *inspires!* I am *so* disappointed in Miss California representing my country, not because she doesn't believe in gay marriage, but because she doesn't *inspire* and she doesn't *unite!* And that is what a Miss California and a Miss USA *should.* And I could *not believe* when she became first runner up! If *that girl* would have won *Miss* USA—California—I would have *gone up* on stage—*I shit you not*—I would have gone up on stage, *snatched* that tiara off her head and run out the door. And then I probably would have been arrested, but you know what? *So be it! Ooooh!* Thank *goodness* Miss South Carolina won—or North Carolina—whichever one won, because she deserved it *so much more!* Okay…I need a cocktail now."

In a subsequent appearance on NBC's *Today Show*, the lovely and gracious Mr. Hilton went on to further elaborate on his open-minded, inclusive philosophy of kindness and tolerance: "I personally would have appreciated it, had she left her *politics* and her religion *out*, because Miss USA represents *all* Americans. I think I gave her the easy way out. She could have answered that question so many different ways. She could have said, 'Well, I wanna leave my *politics* out of the question and I think that it's important for the states to make those decisions for themselves, and I think that would have been a better answer than the one that she gave, because the answer she gave alienated *myself*, millions of gays and lesbians, their friends, their family, their coworkers, and their supporters. And Miss USA is not a person that's alienating. *Miss USA is not a person that's politically incorrect!* Miss USA is someone who represents me, who represents all America and is *inclusive*."

After pausing for a moment of intermission to digest those bits of brilliance and purge any thoughts of Perez Hilton *as* Miss California from our temporarily scarred psyches, we are well served to consider a question of our own: Throughout this incident and the firestorm of controversy that followed, Carrie Prejean's position was painted as suspiciously defensive in most Statist media presentations, while the Perez Hilton position was generally treated as normative and therefore worthy of *less* scrutiny or criticism than Miss Prejean's. Why is this so?

The answer to this question as well as many related issues swirling about the perpetual conspiracy to assassinate Sarah Palin are found in the very nature and identity of the counter-Christian culture in which we live. In an America teetering on the brink of a shift from post-Christian to anti-Christian state, the Secular Inquisition has begun.

WELCOME TO THE SECULAR INQUISITION

If the world hates you, know that it has hated me before it hated you.

JESUS IN JOHN 15:18

All animals are equal, but some animals are more equal than others.

GEORGE ORWELL, *ANIMAL FARM*

While Carrie Prejean's tepid, defensive, limp-wristed (and she didn't even get points for *that*), ever-so polite response to Perez Hilton's question did indeed cost her the title of Miss USA, it also managed to reap a wealth of useful information. However flamboyant a representative of contemporary American leftism Mr. Hilton may be, his views are largely representative of the hyper-relativistic brand of secular humanism that currently dictates the course and rate of decline for our culture. Sadly, Hilton's *is* the favored position, at least from the perspective of the secular forces driving our nation. This makes the Prejean/Hilton exchange worthy of further consideration.

I'd like to begin this examination by offering a list of post-Christian American truths made plain through Perez Hilton's response to Carrie Prejean:

1. Biblically submissive Christians cannot represent America. "All of America" includes ridiculous living caricatures of homosexuality; it does *not* include Bible believing Christians.

2. Biblically submissive Christians *can be excluded* in the name of inclusiveness. Put another way, alienating Christians is perfectly acceptable for the simple reason that they are perceived to alienate others.

3. Political expression is reserved *exclusively* for those expressing politically correct views.

4. Religious expressions, if they must be made at all, are allowed only insofar as they conform completely to anti-Christian standards, thus rendering the Christian silent.

5. Political and religious questions, when asked of a Christian by an anti-Christian, cannot be answered honestly or accurately, as the Christian response must universally conform to anti-Christian standards and is therefore impossible. In this light, anti-Christians really do not ask Christians questions at all—they merely use a question format to *inform* the Christian of truth from an anti-Christian perspective. It's kind of like a satanic twist on *Jeopardy!*

6. So complete is the subjugation of the liberal lemming's mind that they are literally incapable of noticing their own flagrantly religious and political expressions as anything but the completely benign norm for all of humanity. They literally do not realize that *their* opinion is *an* opinion. As

William F. Buckley, Jr. put it, "Liberals claim to want to give a hearing to other views, but then are shocked and offended to discover that there are other views."

7. Expressing an anti-Christian opinion in the promotion of tolerance, acceptance, and unity is a natural and good thing, while expressing a Christian opinion on the same matter is almost always an open violation of goodness and decency at every level.

8. Perez and Paris Hilton are of roughly equal value to western civilization.

There are many more useful points that could be listed, to be sure, but the true nature of the new American thought police is revealed clearly enough by these eight examples. In a nutshell: Bible-believing Christians are, by definition, wrong and must be silenced. This is the guiding principle of the Secular Inquisition.

This movement has been underway in America for some time now. It continues to gather steam, having moved beyond its base of Statist media support and into the deeper fabric of the culture, primarily through the government education system. Its goal is, for now, the silence and suppression of Christian thought. As such, every Common Believer is a threat and legitimate target of the Secular Inquisition.

Any public expression of distinctly Christian thought must be met. It must be countered. It must be crushed. And soon, it must be *banned*.

There are those who would say that the last contention paints an overdramatic picture, that the author here is presenting a skewed take on reality for the sake of promoting alarm and implying the existence of an evil conspiracy against liberty, when in reality there is no such thing to be found. To these critics, we need only reply with a simple point north...to Canada.

THE CRIME OF CHRISTIAN

"In Canada, we respect freedom of speech, but we don't worship it."

CANADIAN BROADCAST STANDARDS COUNCIL

On April 29, 2004, Canada's governor general signed into law a measure that criminalized public expression in opposition to homosexual behavior, officially categorizing some orthodox Christian beliefs, when verbalized publically, as "hate speech." Welcome to the world of tolerance and inclusiveness, Perez Hilton style.

Albert Mohler Jr. addressed this seismic legal and cultural shift in an opinion piece featured at Crosswalk.com titled *The End of Religious Liberty in Canada*[9]:

> It's all over but the funeral. Free speech and religious liberty are now effectively dead in Canada, and recent developments across our northern border should awaken Americans to the peril of political correctness and its restrictions on freedom.
> On April 28, the Canadian Senate passed bill C-250 by a vote of 59 to 11. In passing this legislation, the Canadian Parliament added "sexual orientation" to the nation's laws criminalizing "hate speech." The end result is that the Bible may now be considered a form of criminalized hate literature and Christians who teach that homosexuality is sinful may face criminal charges.

---

[9] *The End of Religious Liberty in Canada* posted at Crosswalk.com
http://www.crosswalk.com/1264412/page0/

This reality is worthy of our pause and careful consideration. The categorization of Bible content as hate speech deserving of punishment, constitutes state-sponsored persecution of Christians. This is what Canada has become.

Dr. Mohler concluded his warning to Christendom with the following:

> The pattern of criminalizing speech about homosexuals is spreading across liberal societies. In Sweden, pastors are explicitly warned that any sermons critical of homosexuality can lead to criminal charges. The same logic is spreading through the courts and legislatures of many European countries—and now has jumped the Atlantic to Canada.
>
> The truly threatening character of the Canadian legislation is further demonstrated in the fact that police do not have to charge persons with breaking a law. Any Canadian citizen can file a complaint against any other citizen, resulting in charges. At that point, the defendant is simply left to the dangerous whims of the liberal judiciary and governmental human rights commissions. The potential legal costs would alone intimidate some persons from talking about homosexuality.
>
> The most important part of the newly-revised criminal code reads: 'Everyone who, by communicating statements, other than in private conversation, willfully promotes hatred against any identifiable group is guilty of...an indictable offense and is liable to imprisonment for a term not exceeding two years.'
>
> During a recent debate, the Canadian attorney general refused to comment on whether or not the Bible is, in itself, hate speech. That matter, we are now warned, will be left for the courts to determined.

We are fooling ourselves if we believe this threat to religious liberty will stay on the Canadian side of the border. This same logic is already accepted by many law professors and judges in the United States. The passage of C-250 is a warning to us all. When free speech is denied and the preachers are told what they can and cannot say, religious liberty is effectively dead.[10]

Man has spoken. The spirit of antichrist and rebellion has spoken. The Canadian thought police have spoken: God's perfect Word on homosexuality is evil and its public proclamation can result in punishment by law.

Liberal fascism is on the march on both sides of the US/Canadian border. The Secular Inquisition is hardly confined by national boundaries. It is a global ideology simultaneously consumed and fueled by its overt hatred of truth and its author. The thought police are on a mission. As they march forward, they aim for nothing less than the total subjugation of our nation to their politically correct code…one individual at a time.

In subsequent chapters, we will further explore many of the numerous individual examples of this stormtrooper-style trampling of liberty. But before we go on to examine the stories of others, I would like to pull our focus back from the far flung fields of the cultural battlefield and into our own communities, homes, and individual lives.

We make this exploration for a purpose: It is vital that we realize our *personal* status as targets of the Secular Inquisition. You and I are anything but immune to this persecution. We are solidly locked

---

[10] *The End of Religious Liberty in Canada* posted at Crosswalk.com
http://www.crosswalk.com/1264412/page0/

into the enemy's crosshairs, each and every one of us, and for this, we must be *thankful*.

Yes, you read correctly. The Common Believer is to be thankful for biblically prescribed persecution.

As our Lord has called us to serve Him completely, He has called us to struggle. This is a price of our obedience to Christ in a God-hating world. This is a burden that our Lord has lovingly empowered us to bear. This is a quality that the Secular Inquisition simply cannot grasp or overcome.

THE PRICE OF CHRISTIANITY

Indeed, all who desire to live a godly life in Christ Jesus will be persecuted, while evil people and impostors will go on from bad to worse, deceiving and being deceived.

2 TIMOTHY 3:12-13

If I had not done among them the works that no one else did, they would not be guilty of sin, but now they have seen and hated both me and my Father.

JESUS IN JOHN 15:24

Contrary to popular opinion, the call to Christianity is not an easy or simple thing to take up. The life of a Common Believer is difficult. *Impossibly* difficult. One of the first realities of Christian life that we are called to embrace is that, as a natural consequence of our living for Christ, we *will* be hated by this world.

This hatred is not optional. It is not avoidable. It's not a mere possibility, likelihood or probability. It is an absolute certainty and as such, it is something to which we should give some thought.

This reality required no explanation or revelation when Christ's church first formed after His earthly ministry. Hatred was the world's reaction to the first Christians. Persecution was as much a part of life for them as was eating or sleeping.

This persecution was not only endured by the first Christians, it was *celebrated*. Those who first promoted the Christian church viewed persecution as an essential beauty and privilege for the believer.

It is in this light that even the Secular Inquisition reveals itself to be an unwitting tool of the God it so despises. By persecuting the Common Believer, as it is fervently committed to do, this movement offers each of us a precious and unique opportunity to glorify our Lord. What a wonderful confirmation this is of Paul's words in the book of Romans:

And we know that for those who love God all things work together for good, for those who are called according to his purpose. (Romans 8:28)

This price of true Christianity also gives us something of a barometer or measuring stick with which we can gauge our spiritual walk. We can know, for example, that if this world simply adores us in all that we say and do, then we are most assuredly *not* living for Christ. This world is in open rebellion against Him, and the more we reflect His will, the more we will be hated for it. This is as simple and clear a truth as any presented in Scripture.

Our reason for celebrating this truth rather than recoiling from it is that persecution from the world always offers the Common Believer a precious opportunity to glorify God that couldn't have come any other way.

These opportunities to glorify God through adversity come not only in direct response to the most flagrant displays of anti-Christian bias and persecution that a Common Believer may experience. They also come as we care for a hurting brother or sister, or as we comfort a non-believing friend in distress. They come as we patiently explain truth to children who struggle to grasp the nature of this world and the world to come. They come as we simply walk and talk with a concerned neighbor. The opportunities to glorify God through this time of cultural upheaval are as numerous as heaven's stars. This should be on our minds always as we endure, persevere, and bring light into a dark and dying world through the blessing of persecution.

THE COMMON BELIEVER'S DAILY OPPORTUNITY

Do your best to present yourself to God as one approved, a worker who has no need to be ashamed, rightly handling the word of truth.

2 TIMOTHY 2:15

Every issue of consequence should inspire in the mind of the Common Believer one simple question: What has God said about this? As we tackle the myriad concepts and ideas associated with the ongoing culture war in America, we must maintain a conscious devotion and fidelity to the Bible. It is our only reliable lifeline. Emotion, tradition, and personal preference cannot be allowed to guide us in any way contrary to Scripture, and resisting such inclinations is no easy thing.

What *is e*asy for us to do is miss or mishandle opportunities to glorify God through our persecution by forgetting the principles at the core of biblical Christianity.

When we encounter the comically incoherent and hypocritical rants of a Perez Hilton or the hateful pronouncements of a Margaret Cho, we have to resist the emotional urge to respond in any number of wrong ways. While we can and must defend truth and, at times, do so in a fiery, passionate manner, we must never forget that these people are only acting according to their nature— *a nature that we shared completely before Christ imposed spiritual life upon us.* So when we face the slings and arrows inherent in culture warfare, we must never presume to operate from a position of moral superiority based upon anything of *our* doing. Our life, strength, purpose, and power have been given to us by Christ, and we must resist every inclination to separate ourselves from this truth in any attempt to stand "on our own two feet." Only through complete reliance upon and submission to our Lord in all things can we avoid the distractions and pitfalls that seek to trip up and trap every Common Believer.

When we observe events like the political frenzy surrounding Sarah Palin or the strange phenomenon that was the Miss California saga, it can be easy to lose sight of the core issues at the heart of all of the drama. It's easy to get lost in the fog of snippets, half-truths, and half-thoughts advertised as useful information in this era of the sound-bite and 24/7 "news" cycle.

We will more quickly find peace and success on the cultural battlefield when we focus on Christ. Common Believers can rest assured in the knowledge that God has provided answers to *every* essential question that we might face. With this knowledge comes responsibility. We cannot experience the true peace or joy He has made available unless we seek His will and *apply* it in our daily lives.

The acquisition of knowledge without the application of that knowledge is of no use at all. Only through submission to His revealed truth can we find true hope, peace, power, and purpose.

As we engage the culture and confront the Secular Inquisition, we are well served to hold close and contemplate the following biblical truths:

1. We are to *expect persecution.*
2. We are to *be thankful for persecution.*
3. We are to *pray for our enemies.*
4. We are to *defend truth.*

Each of these suspiciously simple-sounding points are of great weight and consequence. Each is worthy of lengthy contemplation and requires a life-long commitment to prayerful implementation. But don't let that frighten you off! As expressed earlier, the same Lord who has called us to accomplish these otherwise impossible tasks has also equipped us to do so. In recognition of this most critical and comforting of truths, we will add a fifth point to our list:

5. We *will be sustained and enabled through Christ to accomplish all of these things.*

It is this fifth point that makes the first four possible.

Always remember that the Secular Inquisition sweeping through contemporary American culture is no surprise to God. It was ordained by Him from the very dawn of creation. It is His tool. He *will* use it to His glory and our ultimate benefit.

AND CELEBRATING PERSECUTION

Blessed are those who are persecuted for righteousness sake, for theirs is the kingdom of heaven. Blessed are you when others revile you and persecute you and utter all kinds of evil against you falsely on my account. Rejoice and be glad, for your reward is great in heaven, for so they persecuted the prophets who were before you.

JESUS IN MATTHEW 5:10–11

By lovingly warning us of the certain hatred we will inspire in this fallen world, our Lord has graced us with the opportunity to prepare.

As an essential early step in this preparation, we must come to embrace, however contrary to our nature the concept may seem, the biblical notion that the persecution we are assured to face is ultimately *for our benefit.* When this truth, as expressed by Jesus in Matthew 5:10–11, is fully grasped, the Common Believer's vision is sure to clear and their fear will give way to hope and anticipation. When we take an eternal perspective on persecution and actually come to agree that it is *always* to the glory of God, and therefore to our personal benefit as His people, we are then enabled to pray for our enemies and defend truth much more effectively.

And effective prayer is our greatest weapon in this culture war. As Hank Hanegraaff rightly described it, "Prayer is firing the winning shot."

ACHIEVING SYMPATHY AND EMPATHY THROUGH PRAYER

You have heard that it was said, 'You shall love your neighbor and hate your enemy.' But I say to you, Love your enemies and pray for those who persecute you, so that you may be sons of your Father who is in heaven. For he makes his sun rise on the evil and on the good, and sends rain on the just and on the unjust.

JESUS IN MATTHEW 5:43–45

When we acknowledge that every rebellious, sinful man and woman engaged in the culture war on behalf of the enemies of Christ is only acting according to their nature and that we were once just as they are now, both sympathy and empathy become much easier to sincerely grasp as we heed our Lord's command to pray for those who persecute us.

As each of us reflects upon the state we were in before Christ claimed us as His own, every delusion of self-significance or independent personal capacity for good should evaporate. Hand in glove with this growth in knowledge will also come a heart for the lost so that they might too be found by Him.

This contrite, humble, God-fearing, and Gospel-fueled prayer will shake the world, one life at a time. It will break us of our arrogant notions of self-significance and allow for our transformation into the most effective culture warrior imaginable. The Spirit-filled, prayer-fueled Common Believer is the enemy most feared by the Secular Inquisition, and for the best of reasons.

The fallen world's fear of the Fire Breathing Christian is a most reasonable thing.

SWIM DEEP, MAKE WAVES!

For though by this time you ought to be teachers, you need someone to teach you again the basic principles of the oracles of God. You need milk, not solid food, for everyone who lives on milk is unskilled in the word of righteousness, since he is a child. But solid food is for the mature, for those who have their powers of discernment trained by constant practice to distinguish good from evil.

HEBREWS 5:12–14

For though we walk in the flesh, we are not waging war according to the flesh. For the weapons of our warfare are not of the flesh but have divine power to destroy strongholds. We destroy arguments and every lofty opinion raised against the knowledge of God, and take every thought captive to obey Christ.

2 CORINTHIANS 10:3–5

With the opportunity of persecution upon us, and proper prayer as our fuel, we have been placed by God and prepared by His Word and Spirit for battle. This is where things can get tricky. The challenge for the Common Believer here is great, particularly in a setting such as that presented in the contemporary United States of America. The problem in question is: This will be hard. Very hard.

And hard is not popular these days in America or in American Christendom.

Yet hard is our path and there's absolutely no way around it. There's no shortcut, cheat, secret code, or letter from our parents that can excuse us from the studies we must pursue. There is no gimmick that can free us from this path. There is simply no escape: We *must* study our Bibles.

The purpose of this book is not to offer you a three-step plan to biblical literacy. You will find no magical acronym or memorization techniques promoted here, though I certainly do encourage memorization. The one thing that I would like to focus on and advocate in this book is as simple as it is difficult: individual effort.

There is nothing remotely similar in its ability to positively impact the life of a Common Believer. Sheer time and effort spent in and on the Word of God cannot be compensated for by any other activity. Only the dedicated pursuit of biblical knowledge will bring us the depth of understanding we require for personal growth so that we might engage the culture and claim victory for the Kingdom of Christ.

There is no workaround for this. It must be done "the hard way." That's the bad news.

The good news is that when you personally cross the threshold from *having* to study to *wanting* to study—and that day will come—you'll look back on even this bit of "bad news" as having been one of the most wonderful things to have ever come your way. As we mature and begin to actually grasp the individual sense of peace, joy and purpose already mentioned time and time again, we will come to celebrate that "bad news." As our hopes for what a Christian life *should* be become realized through the daily study and application of His Word, we will better understand and cherish the sentiments of Paul as he wrote to the church at Ephesus:

*"And he gave the apostles, the prophets, the evangelists, the shepherds and teachers, **to equip the saints for the work of ministry,** for building up the body of Christ, until we all attain to the unity of the faith and of the knowledge of the Son of God, to mature manhood, to the measure of the stature of the fullness of Christ, **so that we may no longer be children, tossed to and fro by the waves and carried about by every wind of doctrine, by human cunning, by craftiness in deceitful schemes."*

EPHESIANS 4:11–14 (emphasis added)

When the Common Believer is equipped in this manner, an unstoppable soldier has just taken to the field of battle. With our eyes on Christ and our minds on His Word, we can accomplish anything...and we will.

When we face the raging storm of this culture war with our eyes firmly fixed on Jesus, we have nothing to fear. When we have nothing to fear, *we* can dictate the terms of engagement. When we dictate the terms of engagement, we proclaim and live truth rather than merely reacting to evil. All of this is made possible for each and every Common Believer and these are the things that make the culture war not only something that we can endure, but something that we can be thankful for as we engage, overcome, and bring Glory to God throughout the process.

As for the Secular Inquisition? Bring 'em on! They'll never know what hit 'em.

21

THE GOD WHO STRUTS

IT'S ALL ABOUT HIM

"God is the only comfort, He is also the supreme terror: the thing we most need and the thing we most want to hide from."

C.S. LEWIS

"If you find God with great ease, perhaps it is not God that you have found."

THOMAS MERTON

Before my parents divorced, we lived in an old farmhouse. I was four. I remember sitting out on the porch one day with my dad. We were sitting side-by-side, looking up at the sky and talking about God.

He said he could see His footprints up there in the clouds. His eyes were locked in a fixed gaze upwards. He was definitely focused on *something* up there as he spoke and I was convinced that God must right at that particular moment be walking amongst those particular clouds. What a privilege to have Him so close, I thought. I only wished that I could see Him, too.

When I was a little boy, I thought that people naturally wanted to find God. Now I know better.

HOLY TERROR

And the four living creatures, each of them with six wings, are full of eyes all around and within, and day and night they never cease to say, **"Holy, holy, holy, is the Lord God Almighty, who was and is and is to come!"**

REVELATION 4:8 (bold emphasis mine)

And I said: "Woe is me! For I am lost; for I am a man of unclean lips, and I dwell in the midst of a people of unclean lips; for my eyes have seen the King, the LORD of hosts!"

ISAIAH 6:5

There are, at this very moment, the most peculiar and magnificent of angelic creatures circling the throne of God. They sing without end or interruption of our Lord's defining attribute: His perfect holiness.

202

They do not tire. They neither relent nor regret.

They somehow even manage to resist the most terrible scourge of our age: boredom. Where we cannot imagine tolerating, much less desiring, such an existence, they yearn for nothing else. Nothing less than audibly proclaiming the holiness of God even appeals to them.

This is the task for which they were made: To endlessly announce God's perfect holiness. He made them for this purpose, and that truth alone tells us much about Him, if we'll let it.

Hundreds of years before John the Revelator was granted a vision of these amazing six-winged heralds of God's majesty, the prophet Isaiah had a momentous encounter with one of them.

The creature approached Isaiah just after he had beheld the holiness of God. In that instant, having been confronted with his own complete depravity in light of the Lord's perfect holiness, Isaiah utterly unraveled and collapsed, proclaiming, "Woe is me! For I am lost; for I am a man of unclean lips, and I dwell in the midst of a people of unclean lips; for my eyes have seen the King, the LORD of hosts!"

R.C. Sproul described the encounter this way:

> "We are fortunate in one respect: God does not appear to us in the way He appeared to Isaiah. Who could stand it? God normally reveals our sinfulness to us a bit at a time. We experience a gradual recognition of our own corruption. God showed Isaiah his corruption all at once. No wonder he was ruined.
>
> Isaiah explained it this way: "My eyes have seen the King, the LORD Almighty" (Isa. 6:5). He saw the holiness of God. For the first time in his life Isaiah really understood who God was. At the same instant, for the first time Isaiah really understood who Isaiah was.

Then one of the seraphs flew to me with a live coal in his hand, which he had taken with tongs from the altar. With it he touched my mouth and said, "See, this has touched your lips; your guilt is taken away and your sin atoned for."
(Isaiah 6:6–7)

Isaiah was groveling on the floor. . . The seraph pressed the white-hot coal to the lips of the prophet and seared him. . . He was refined by holy fire.

In this divine act of cleansing, Isaiah experienced a forgiveness that went beyond the purification of his lips. He was cleansed throughout, forgiven to the core, but not without the awful pain of repentance. He went beyond the cheap grace and the easy utterance "I'm sorry." He was in mourning for his sin, overcome with moral grief, and God sent an angel to heal him. His sin was taken away. His dignity remained intact. His guilt was removed, but his humanity was not insulted. The conviction that he felt was constructive. His was no cruel and unusual punishment. A second of burning flesh on the lips brought a healing that would extend to eternity. In a moment, the disintegrated prophet was whole again. His mouth was purged. He was clean."[11]

Once Isaiah had an accurate understanding of his own wretched nature and his Lord's perfect holiness *imposed* upon him, and the infinite gap between God and the "holiest" of men was made plain, he was fully prepared for service. Then God used him.

---

[11] R.C. Sproul, *The Holiness of God* (Tyndale, 1998), p. 30-31

HOLY, HOLY, HOLY

And I heard the voice of the Lord saying, "Whom shall I send, and who will go for us?" Then I said, "Here am I! Send me."

ISAIAH 6:8

"God saved you for Himself; God saved you by Himself; God saved you from Himself."

PAUL WASHER

"God doesn't choose those who would choose Him. He chooses those who would never choose Him."

MARK DRISCOLL

Our God is holy. We are on the opposite end of the spectrum…in every way and without exception. When Isaiah was made to understand these things, he was transformed.

In all of Scripture, there is not an attribute of the Lord more emphasized or highlighted than that of His holiness. When we view His every other identifiable attribute with this over-arching holiness as a guiding light, we better understand any characteristic under consideration and, as a result, increase in right knowledge of Him.

The seraphim do not sing *Love, love, love!* They sing *Holy, holy, holy!* This is not accidental.

God *is* love, insofar as we understand this as *holy* love. Of course, the love of God tends to bear little resemblance to this fallen world's numerous redefinitions, reincarnations, and repudiations of the biblical concept. It is important to note that the same world that has so radically redefined the notion of love would very much like to have us focus on any of the resultant soft counterfeits as our guiding principle when we seek togain a better understanding of God and His truth. This is a temptation that we must not only resist, but refute whenever and wherever we find it lurking about.

How many times have you heard God's *holy* wrath questioned, disputed, or openly refuted because "God is love" and that such a thing as this "holy wrath" deal is simply incompatible with love? The same is often said of God's *holy* justice, His *holy* vengeance, His *holy* discipline, and His *holy* jealousy.

These perversions and slight-of-mind tricks aside, God's perfect love is and must always be understood as holy love, just as his wrath is always holy wrath, his jealousy is always holy jealousy, and his judgment is always holy judgment. God is not held to man's standards on any subject at any time. God is the author, origin, and continually sustaining source of all of these things. God owes man no explanation. God, in short, is God.

God *defines* what is good and true simply by His actions, which are the demonstration of His will.

God's love is *not* soft. It is not easy. It is perfect. It is *holy*.

Once we rightly understand this, we will not merely accept it. We will celebrate it as nothing else. When we celebrate the fact that God, and *only* God, is capable of this perfectly holy love, wrath, jealousy, and justice, we are then made able, willing, and even eager to fully and completely trust in the sheer perfection of His nature as our very sustenance. Only then can we accept and ultimately celebrate what is, to this fallen world, the most terrifying attribute of our holy God: His complete sovereignty.

THE GOD WHO STRUTS THROUGH SCRIPTURE

"O the depths of the riches both of the wisdom and knowledge of God! how unsearchable are His judgments, and His ways past finding out"

ROMANS 11:33

Imagine, if you will, the following game-show scenario: The production features ten intelligent, honest, and sincere adults. These people, though they are very well educated in every other area of inquiry, have absolutely no knowledge of the Bible or Christianity whatsoever. One last bit of info on our ten hypothetical folks: They have a perfect understanding of language. They are literally unencumbered by any weakness in this area.

Now, let's imagine these ten intellectual and linguistic freaks of nature are summoned to appear on our game show. Or maybe it's more like a "challenge show" in that there is a prize offered for doing an immense amount of detailed research in solitude and then correctly answering simple, clear questions pertaining to the subject under consideration.

No tricks or trick questions. No gimmicks. No wacky, out-of-the blue surprises or peculiar angles to be played. Just simple, clear answers to equally simple, unambiguous questions.

Now, imagine that these lucky boys and girls are each individually sequestered for as long as it takes them to thoroughly read through the Bible. Then, having just methodically read through it for the very first time, and without exposure to outside sources or contaminants of any sort, they are asked to answer four simple questions about Christianity based exclusively on what they had just read:

1. How did our world come into being?
2. What was "the fall"?
3. Who is Jesus?
4. Who determines salvation for each individual member of fallen mankind?

Our ten participants are not required to agree with or evaluate the concepts under consideration. They are merely asked to explain what this religion's sacred book has to say on the matters. Nothing more; nothing less.

If the potential of a ginormous cash payout would help to emphasize the point here, feel free to imagine a multi-million dollar windfall promised to any of the ten who are able to give simple, clear, and accurate responses to each of these four questions.

As Christians, we expect clear and unified responses to these questions. At least the middle two, anyway.

"The Fall" was the fall of mankind through the original sin of Adam's disobedience of God. This transgression plunged the human race and all of creation into its current darkened state. This basic description would surely be the unanimous position taken by our ten participants, and on that point we'd all agree, too. Similarly, Jesus would be rightly identified as God—the Word made flesh; the exclusive Savior, come into the world so that He might bear the price of sin that had submerged humanity into its depraved state. Unanimous harmony on this answer as well would be the clear expectation of every Christian viewer of this particular game-show.

But when it comes to those bookend questions, we run into some trouble. Not trouble with the ten participants. Nope, they will each still provide completely harmonious and unanimous answers where the first and fourth questions are concerned. The problem is with the Christian audience.

You see, the Christian audience would *not* agree on the answers to those two questions at all, no matter how complete the harmony was amongst the game-show participants.

THE GOD WHO STRUTS UNENCUMBERED

And we know that for those who love God all things work together for good, for those who are called according to his purpose. For those whom he foreknew he also predestined to be conformed to the image of his Son, in order that he might be the firstborn among many brothers. And those whom he predestined he also called, and those whom he called he also justified, and those whom he justified he also glorified.

ROMANS 8:28–30

Having read through the Bible and emerged unencumbered by any personal tradition, habit or outside interference, these ten would each answer questions one and four as follows:

Q1. How did our world come into being?
A1. God made it in six literal days.
Q4. Who determines salvation for each member of fallen mankind?
A4. God does, and He does so alone.

Having read the Bible, and only the Bible, and with millions of bucks on the line, I might add, these ten people would be thankful for the clarity in those pages on even these two subjects. They would have no trouble at all providing these answers, and with total confidence in their accuracy.

Money in the bank, they would think. And they'd be right.

With no pet tradition to steer them and no outside whispers in their ear to explain why the book they just read doesn't actually mean what it so clearly said (there's that "did God *really* say?" deal again), these good people would consider their multi-million dollar paydays in the bag, so to speak. Especially since, as we've already covered, they are not being asked to affirm or agree with these sentiments at all. All they have to do is accurately express what the written word says. That's all.

Of course, were they required to express only interpretations of this new-to-them Scripture that they *agreed* with, well, that's a whole 'nother story. With that significant change of rules in place, we could expect significant divergence between the ten answers provided. Kind of like the division we find in the Christian audience.

While some would maintain the same positions expressed in Scenario #1, there would be many—almost certainly a majority— who would not. They would feel compelled to mold the creation account in Genesis 1 to conform with contemporary scientific postulates and theories. The Genesis record would be dismissed as a mere "story."

Similarly, many of these folks would have no interest whatsoever in acknowledging, much less claiming, a God who owned them so completely. They'd want nothing to do with a God so total in His sovereignty ("total sovereignty" being redundant, of course), that *He* would be the determiner of *their* fates. Thus, Romans 9, John 6, and countless other crystal clear proclamations of God's uncompromised sovereignty over *all* things would be radically modified in their minds, or jettisoned altogether.

It's important to note that, in all likelihood, question one, on the matter of creation, would inspire less controversy than question four. The reason for this is that question four completely impacts each and every person considering it in a manner that is comprehensive. It hits the macro and it hits the micro...and completely on both counts. It is both worldview and personal identity defining in its nature. Being told that one is not the center of the universe—or even the central figure in determining their own fate—is not something that one will, of his own volition or nature, *ever* embrace.

Which is precisely why God has to impose upon us even the ability to do *that*. Remember: Before He did that very thing for each of us on an individual basis at a specific moment in time, each and every Common Believer was in that sovereignty-rejecting boat. That was our nature. It was who we were.

During the answer section for question four—the portion of our show where contestants give voice to their answers to the questions put to them—we'd witness the full fury of indignant human opposition to the very notion of a sovereign God. We'd be treated to rants about "robots," "puppets," "free will," and the ultimate expression of outrage regarding the clear pronouncement of Scripture on the matter of predestination: "But that's...*not...fair!*"

God's response to this? Boo. And Hoo.

I am, of course, paraphrasing. His actual Word on the subject are much more abrasive and challenging.

THE GOD WHO OWNS YOUR WILL

But the LORD hardened the heart of Pharaoh, and he did not listen to them, as the LORD had spoken to Moses.

Then the LORD said to Moses, "Rise up early in the morning and present yourself before Pharaoh and say to him, 'Thus says the LORD, the God of the Hebrews, "Let my people go, that they may serve me. For this time I will send all my plagues on you yourself,-and on your servants and your people, so that you may know that there is none like me in all the earth. For by now I could have put out my hand and struck you and your people with pestilence, and youwould have been cut off from the earth. But for this purpose I have raised you up, to show you my power, so that my name may be proclaimed in all the earth.

EXODUS 9:12–16

Our God is sovereign. Completely sovereign.

As He is the only being capable of holy perfection in all things at all times, we must celebrate the notion that He is also *complete* in His sovereignty over all things at all times. Any lesser view of God's sovereign control always has catastrophic results. This was, it should be noted, the prevailing view of Christians who founded the first colonies in the now-United States of America as well as most of those who actualized the American Revolution.

This is no small thing. It is not coincidental.

The fact that the Reformation, the Pilgrims, and the American Revolution are so closely linked by this very *specific* Christianity is one great key to our understanding how and why we have fallen as a nation, as well as how we might be revived. History declares that this high view of God and low view of man was an essential component to both the Reformation and Revolution. It is therefore only reasonable to expect that this view is an essential ingredient for any genuine, lasting American renewal.

This God saves. He saves completely and without fail. He never "tries" to do anything.

This God is sovereign over every action befalling or taken by any creature that He has made:

Are not two sparrows sold for a penny? And not one of them will fall to the ground apart from your Father. (MATTHEW 10:29)

This God is sovereign over every roll of the dice:

The lot is cast into the lap, but its every decision is from the LORD. (PROVERBS 16:33)

There is no randomness in this God's cosmos. Nothing is left to chance. Nothing happens outside of His purpose. This God even uses *apparently* random devices to secure significant decisions as a part of His perfect plan:

And they cast lots for them, and the lot fell on Matthias, and he was numbered with the eleven apostles. (ACTS 1:26)

This God is sovereign over the hearts of men:

The king's heart is a stream of water in the hand of the LORD; he turns it wherever he will. (PROVERBS 21:1)

This God has crafted everything and everyone, including the wicked, for a specific purpose:

The LORD has made everything for its purpose, even the wicked for the day of trouble. (PROVERBS 16:4)

This God is sovereign over every step that every man takes in life:

A man's steps are from the LORD; how then can man understand his way? (PROVERBS 20:24)

This God is sovereign over every human will, even regarding that man's salvation:
So then it depends not on human will or exertion, but on God, who has mercy. (ROMANS 9:16)

This God is sovereign over every ruler or person of power, be they evil or good. He makes them and uses them for His purposes. They are His tools; His property. Yes, even Michael Moore. He lifts them up and brings them down all according to His will in pursuit of His perfect, self-glorifying plan:

For the Scripture says to Pharaoh, "For this very purpose I have raised you up, that I might show my power in you, and that my name might be proclaimed in all the earth." (ROMANS 9:17)

This God is sovereign over who will receive His mercy and who will not:

So then he has mercy on whomever he wills, and he hardens whomever he wills. (ROMANS 9:18)

This God commands dead men to rise from their graves, and they always obey:

[Jesus] cried with a loud voice, Lazarus, come forth. And he that was dead came forth... (JOHN 11:43–44)

This God slays those who steal His glory:

"Immediately an angel of the Lord struck him down, because he did not give God the glory, and he was eaten by worms and breathed his last." (ACTS 12:23)

This God sends delusions to men, so that they will not believe what is true and be condemned:

Therefore God sends them a strong delusion, so that they may believe what is false, in order that all may be condemned who did not believe the truth but had pleasure in unrighteousness. (2 THESSALONIANS 2:11–12)

This God is the sovereign determiner over *all* things, including the eternal state of every individual:

But it is not as though the word of God has failed. For not all who are descended from Israel belong to Israel, and not all are children of Abraham because they are his offspring, but "Through Isaac shall your offspring be named." This means that it is not the children of the flesh who are the children of God, but the children of the promise are counted as offspring. For this is what the promise said: "About this time next year I will return, and Sarah shall have a son." And not only so, but also when Rebekah had conceived children by one man, our forefather Isaac, though they were not yet born and had done nothing either good or bad—in order that God's purpose of election might continue, not because of works but because of him who calls—she was told, "The older will serve the younger." As it is written, "Jacob I loved, but Esau I hated." (ROMANS 9:6–13)

And right on cue, this God demonstrates His sovereignty even over our own silly questions, as He anticipates our favorite ("But that's not fair!") right here:

What shall we say then? Is there injustice on God's part? By no means! For he says to Moses, "I will have mercy on whom I have mercy, and I will have compassion on whom I have compassion." (ROMANS 9:14–15)

We really hate that part. Until He chooses to regenerate us, that is. It's bad enough that He's sovereign, but He comes across as such a smart-alecky sovereign when He answers our questions before we even ask them. How rude!

But then again, as I paraphrased earlier: Boo and Hoo.

Sovereigns do what they want to do. They *always* get their way. That's what sovereign means. Before one is regenerated, they hate even the thought of this. Afterward…they adore it. Now, back to this (hopefully less) uncomfortable sovereignty thing.

Another annoyingly anticipated question answered in advance by God the Holy Spirit in the book of Romans comes when Paul records the following:

You will say to me then, "Why does he still find fault? For who can resist his will?" But who are you, O man, to answer back to God? Will what is molded say to its molder, "Why have you made me like this?" Has the potter no right over the clay, to make out of the same lump one vessel for honorable use and another for dishonorable use? What if God, desiring to show his wrath and to make known his power, has endured with much patience vessels of wrath prepared for destruction, in order to make known the riches of his glory for vessels of mercy, which he has prepared beforehand for glory—even us whom he has called, not from the Jews only but also from the Gentiles? As indeed he says in Hosea, "Those who were not my people I will call 'my people,' and her who was not beloved I will call 'beloved.'" "And in the very place where it was said to them, 'You are not my people,' there they will be called 'sons of the living God.'" (ROMANS 9:19–26)

Barrack Hussein Obama has his "obscure passages from Romans," and, sadly, the professing church in America has hers. Both sets find themselves dismissed by willful men. Sometimes with a disdainful chuckle or diligently crafted philosophical work-arounds, but dismissed nonetheless.

It really isn't very hard to understand why this particular God is so intensely unpopular, is it? After all, who naturally tolerates, much less aspires to, the notion of being the wholly owned property and tool of another from even before their conception?

Nobody I know.

Yet that is what each and every one of us are: God's tools to be used for His purpose on His schedule in pursuit of His self-glorification. Put another way: It's all about Him. And the "it" in question is *everything*, including us.

Talk about *this* God even in the presence of many sincere professing Christians and you are almost sure to get a particular response: "I could never worship *that* kind of God!"

And, left to our own devices, none of us could. That's the point.

None of us could worship that God...unless He made us able to do so, against our natural, fallen will, by imposing upon us a *new* nature—a nature that *wanted* Him as opposed to hating Him; a nature that could not live without Him. Of our own accord, we are utterly repulsed by such a God as He. Only when He regenerates our fallen nature, bringing it from death to life, can we then recognize and instinctively desire the God of biblical Christianity.

This is the God who, when He is described accurately, will always inspire one of two things in a man: Peace or terror.

For the Common Believer, this God *is* peace.

THE GOD WHO STRUTS THROUGH PROPHECY

And when they heard it, they lifted their voices together to
God and said, "Sovereign Lord, who made the heaven and
the earth and the sea and everything in them, who through
the mouth of our father David, your servant, said by the Holy
Spirit, "'Why did the Gentiles rage, and the peoples plot in
vain? The kings of the earth set themselves, and the rulers
were gathered together, against the Lord and against his
Anointed'—for truly in this city there were gathered together
against your holy servant Jesus, whom you anointed, both
Herod and Pontius Pilate, along with the Gentiles and the
peoples of Israel, to do whatever your hand and your plan
had predestined to take place."

ACTS 4:24–28

Ever since I was a little kid, I've been fascinated by Bible
prophecy. I think that this is a fairly typical, and a very good,
thing. For me, early thoughts on the subject were greatly colored
by Hollywood lunacy (thank you, Damien) and Christian quackery
(hello, Hal Lindsey).

From *Rosemary's Baby* to *Left Behind*, there has been a wide
range of material produced in recent decades where the subject of
eschatology is concerned. While the spectrum of opinions on the
subjects of Christ's return or "the end times" is large, and the
products produced by the minds subscribing to any of them range
from the sublime to the ridiculous, there does seem to be one
essential component in any right understanding of biblical
prophecy.

Perhaps the one and only thing that *is* crystal clear where Bible
prophecy is concerned is this: God must be sovereign over
everything, including, obviously, the will of every man, woman

and child, in order for these detailed prophecies to be 100% fulfilled 100% of the time. Otherwise, with a less impactful God, and more impactful men, the whole thing just wouldn't fly. How could it?

THE SOVEREIGN SUSTAINER OF ISRAEL

"I will make a covenant of peace with them. It shall be an everlasting covenant with them. And I will set them in their land and multiply them, and will set my sanctuary in their midst forevermore. My dwelling place shall be with them, and I will be their God, and they shall be my people. Then the nations will know that I am the LORD who sanctifies Israel, when my sanctuary is in their midst forevermore."

EZEKIEL 37:26–28

Back in the day when I taught Sunday school for the teens at Henderson First Baptist, I remember dedicating a month to discussing the miraculous fact of modern Israel. I found it then, as I do now, to be one of the most compelling arguments for a sovereign God fulfilling the prophecies of His Word. Israel has always been an incomparable beauty to me in that regard.

Yet, like many a modern Christian treatment of the crystal clear Genesis account of creation, there are those who have invented ways around accepting the fact of Israel as presented in the Bible. Most of these dismissals came in the years preceding 1948, when the very thought of an actual nation of Israel re-emerging in the Holy Land was viewed by most as flat out crazy. Nothing like the complete dispersal and subsequent reconstitution of an intact culture had ever happened before in all of human history. This fact of history impacted many Christians of the past in much the same manner that current claims of science impact the thoughts of many regarding the Genesis account of creation. To put it bluntly, where there were serious, substantial and unavoidable conflicts apparent between worldly and biblical pronouncements on these matters, many professing Christians simply opted for the worldly option over the biblical.

It was *so* much easier to go that route…for now, anyway.

Where Genesis was relegated to "story" or "metaphor" or some similarly ridiculous thing, God's chosen nation of Israel was "spiritualized" away. While the temptation to yield to the pressure to spiritualize what must have seemed impossible to most living in the time leading up to World War II is at least understandable in some ways, there are still those in the church who embrace and advocate this view today.

Yet, there she stands: God's chosen nation, Israel.

We really have fallen far when it comes to underestimating the unqualified nature of God's sovereignty. So bad has it become that we can't even acknowledge His sovereign hand *after* it has been so completely revealed in a matter. How weird is that?

OMNIPOTENCE + OMNISCIENCE + OMNIPRESENCE = UNQUALIFIED SOVEREIGNTY

"Providence is a soft pillow."

OLD PURITAN SAYING

Among the first things I remember learning about God were "the three omnis." God is, we are rightly told, omnipotent, omniscient, and omnipresent. These three attributes are typically summarized as:

1. His omnipotence—God controls all things directly; He is all-powerful. There is nothing that derives its power at any time from any source apart from God.
2. His omnipresence—All of creation exists in the direct presence of God. He is always active over all things in every location and in every moment of time.
3. His omniscience—God knows all things, and He knows them completely. As He has brought them into being by His power (a power they are constantly dependent upon), they must completely serve His purpose and are therefore completely known to Him.

God transcends time. This is important. It's an easy thing for us puny little time-based creatures to forget, but it is critical that we keep this concept front and center as we consider the three omnis.

God's omnipresence obviously includes all of time. As He transcends any limitations of time, He can be rightly described as, from our perspective, equally present in all times at the same time. And now my head hurts. I'm sorry if yours does too, but that's just a natural consequence of this sort of subject matter. Yet, on we must trudge.

God's omnipotence also transcends time. He therefore has complete power over every past, present, and future thing. His power—the only self-sufficient power—sustains them all.

God's omniscience then is a natural function of His omnipotence and omnipresence. All things are created by a God equally present in all times, equally defined and sustained by His power, all exclusively for His purpose and glory. This is how we get perfect Bible prophecy, among other things.

The convergence of the three omnis can produce nothing less than a completely sovereign God. For the Common Believer, this is news wonderful beyond description. For the non-believer, it is a most terrible truth.

THE GOD WHO STRUTS THROUGH AMERICAN HISTORY

"If the average American citizen were asked, who was the founder of America, the true author of our great Republic, he might be puzzled to answer. We can imagine his amazement at hearing the answer given to this question by the famous German historian, Ranke, one of the profoundest scholars of modern times. Says Ranke, 'John Calvin was the virtual founder of America.'"

DR. E.W. SMITH

"The Pilgrims who left their country in the reign of James 1, and landing on the barren soil of New England, founded populous and mighty colonies, were his sons, his direct and legitimate sons; and that American nation which we have seen growing so rapidly boasts as its father the humble Reformer on the shore of Lake Leman."

JEAN-HENRI D'AUBIGNÉ

God's sovereign hand guides all of human history. It often makes itself so plain that one must look away and close his eyes in order to miss it. Which is precisely what fallen men are prone to do. Our own nation's history is uniquely intertwined with the biblical belief in and reliance upon a completely sovereign God.

Nearly 500 years ago, the bride of Christ was rescued through the Protestant Reformation. Shortly thereafter, the Reformation-minded Pilgrims came to America.

Nearly 250 years ago, the American Revolution changed the course of world history. Again, this was a movement spearheaded and supported first and foremost by those who openly embraced the biblically submissive spirit of the Reformation and confessed open allegiance to a completely sovereign God.

In between these two grand events came the establishment of various Christian denominations. The Westminster Confession of Faith (1646) and London Baptist Confession (1689) defined the religion that would seed and then give birth to the United States of America.

What do you see here? Purpose or coincidence? Providence or chance?

What if there is a connection between a faith obsessed with the proclamation of a sovereign God and the greatest moments and triumphs of Western Civilization?

What if there are no accidents?

What if God doesn't play dice? At all.

And what if He doesn't *really* let anyone else play either?

What if God is *that* sovereign. You know, like the Bible says.

Would you feel cheated or comforted? Insulted or inspired?

Could knowing and embracing this *particular* God be the key to everything from your own personal peace to a new American Revolution or cultural reformation?

If not, then I suppose that the man-obeying god of our age is the best shot we have, which is another way of saying, "no shot at all."

If so, then He is the *only* key to *any* good thing, be it personal, national, or global.

THE INDENIABLE, IRRESISTIBLE **I AM**

Let all the earth fear the LORD; let all the inhabitants of the world stand in awe of him!

PSALM 33:8

When Jesus walked the planet, He exercised authority over every facet of His creation:

He changed the nature of animals when He rode on a donkey that had never been sat on, making it gentle and subservient (Luke 19:30-35).

He changed the nature of fish when He caused them to jump into the nets (John 21:6).

He changed the nature of water when He caused it to become wine (John 2).

He changed the nature of storms when He caused them to cease with just a word (Matthew 8:25-26).

He changed the nature of a budding fig tree when He caused it to wither and die by His word (Matthew 21:18-20).

He would have changed the nature of stones and caused them to cry out, had the people been silenced (Luke 19:40).

There is no difference when Christ works in the hearts of men. When the Sovereign Lord speaks, His creation obeys Him.

JIM MCCLARTY[12]

Only when we cry "woe" as Isaiah did will we be empowered to accept and adore the truth about the story in which we live: That it is not about us. This amazing tale—the story of creation and all therein—has been written for the purpose of God making each of His holy attributes known. It is a story of His self-expression for the purpose of His self-glorification. It is all about *Him*.

---

[12] Jim McClarty, *By Grace Alone*
(http://www.salvationbygrace.org/uc/sub/docs/bygracealone.pdf)

Only when we embrace our true place in His creation and celebrate *His* free will over it will we finally find ourselves able to fully join in Job's proclamation: "The Lord gives and the Lord takes away. Blessed be the name of the Lord!"

Only when we bask unrestrained in the magnificence of His sovereignty will we come to find the "abundant life" promised to His own. With egos completely surrendered, our once precious desire for some measure of power over God—even if only for an instant or only over one decision—will simply fade away. We will celebrate what we once abhorred. All by His decree. All to our benefit.

We are all His tools; His wholly owned property. For the Common Believer, this is bliss. For the non-believer, it is an affront to their self-perceived dignity—an offensive and horrible proposition of the highest (or lowest) order.

No man "makes Jesus Lord" of anything. Christ is, has always been, and ever shall be the Lord over *every* man.

He requests nothing from man, as He owns all.

He learns nothing from man, as He knows all.

He doesn't need any man's validation or permission to do anything at any time.

He benefits nothing from man; He is completely self-sustaining and self-fulfilling. His state cannot know improvement; it is perfect.

His call is completely effectual; it *always* succeeds in summoning His sheep while repelling goats.

He is not merely the *most* powerful, He is the *All* Powerful.

There are none who have the power to oppose His will because He has *all* of the power. The math of it isn't tricky at all: None have the power to effectively oppose Him precisely because He holds *all* power in His hand and will use every bit of it for His self-glorifying purposes.

This power concept is critical, and it really is a 100% God, 0% everybody else proposition. Grasping that fact alone will go a long way towards guiding us to a right understanding of the God we serve.

He is *All* Mighty. This God *is* God.

What could be more relevant than that? And what could possibly be more comforting to the Common Believer?

When we struggle, flounder and fall, *He is sovereign.*

When we doubt, *He is sovereign.*

When we weep, *He is sovereign.*

When we lose our every possession, *He is sovereign.*

When we are maligned, mocked and persecuted, *He is sovereign.*

When we wage His war and suffer every consequence, *He is sovereign.*

When we see our cherished loved ones snatched away in the prime of their lives, *He is sovereign.*

And because He is sovereign, *all* things—every item and event—in His creation are purposeful by *His* design. There are no accidents. There is no coincidence. There is no chance and nothing is random. Every single solitary thing, thought, and action is gloriously purposeful. Every tear that we shed; every pain that we endure; every tragedy that befalls us; every great and small mistake that we make—each of these things are *completely* purposeful. They have meaning and it is an *intended* meaning; a perfect, purposeful place in the eternal plan of God.

He said so. That's enough to make it so, since, as you might have picked up by now, *He is sovereign.*

And He is a consuming fire… *"FIRE…God of Abraham, the God of Isaac, the God of Jacob, and not of the philosophers and savants. Certitude. Feeling. Joy. Peace."*

He is certitude. He is Joy. And He is peace to the Common Believer. All by way of His undeniable, incontrovertible, unquestionable, and complete *sovereignty.*

He is why our security is certain.

He is why our victory is assured and was *never* in question.

He is the God who struts and flaunts and perfectly displays His majesty through every inclination and move of every part and particle of His creation. And we, of all people, wouldn't want it any other way.

According to His purpose, *He* chose *us*.

Why? That's *His* business. Who are *you*? Besides the former God-hating reprobate who *He* chose to raise from spiritual death to life, I mean? Whatever your answer, I invite you, one former God-hating reprobate to another, to simply join me in surrendering any pretense of cooperative contribution to our salvation and praise Him for doing it *all*.

Why did He choose me? I have no idea. I'm just glad to be here.

This God inspires each of His own in different ways, but always for the same purpose: His. It is *this* God who gives hope; a hope sustained not by our will or ability, but a hope defined by His will and made alive by His almighty power. This God was once the focus of our hearts, our families, our churches, and yes, even our nation. And it can be so again.

If you have read these words and He has used them in their weakness to move or inspire you towards Him, then you probably feel, as I do, that He is even now raising up vessels throughout our land for the purpose of reformation, revival, and restoration. Change is indeed coming to America.

All by His purpose. All for His glory. All as He ordained from the foundation of the world.

This is the God we serve, and His is the Gospel we are called to proclaim—the Gospel for which the martyrs gave their lives and the Gospel that may soon require the same of us.

His is the Gospel for which we will be hated and by which we will know eternal life. His is the Gospel for which we cannot suffer compromise.

This is the time for which we were made.

ACKNOWLEDGMENTS

I thank God for the temporary country and homeland that I now know and love, America, and doubly so for my *true* country and homeland, the perfect Kingdom that has come to conquer all others, and the mission that He has given me in the former 'til the latter finally fully blooms.

I thank Him for my beautiful bride-to-be, Miss Holly Monroe. She is a matchless inspiration and encouragement to me. Her patience, kindness, and supportive input has been priceless. I can only imagine what a wonderful helper she will be in our future life together. God is so good!

I also thank Him for three other godly, patriotic women who have played unique roles in forming and encouraging this book and its mission: Ruth (aka "Gram"), Trina, and Jan. Each of these three women have been an inspiration...and two of the three have even volunteered for proof reading duty!

I thank God for the hopeful signs and apparent sparks of true, Christ-centered reformation, revival, and revolution in America, and I thank every Brother and Sister in Him for their prayers and actions to that end.

May God bless America with that revolution.

231

ABOUT THE AUTHOR

Photograph Copyright 2012 Cali Ashton Photography, Nashville, TN

Scott Alan Buss is a wretch saved by grace, a husband to Holly, and father to Rosie and Wolfgang. He and his family make their home in Middle Tennessee, where he is a thankful member of Christ the King Church.

Scott is a writer, speaker, and the founder of R3V Press, where he has published several books. He regularly blogs and podcasts at *Fire Breathing Christian*.

www.FireBreathingChristian.com

From the author of *Fire Breathing Christians* and *Apathetic Christianity*

SATAN'S

JACKASS

THE PROGRESSIVE PARTY'S
WAR ON CHRISTIANITY

BY SCOTT ALAN BUSS

www.FireBreathingChristian.com

ALSO FROM R3VOLUTION PRESS:

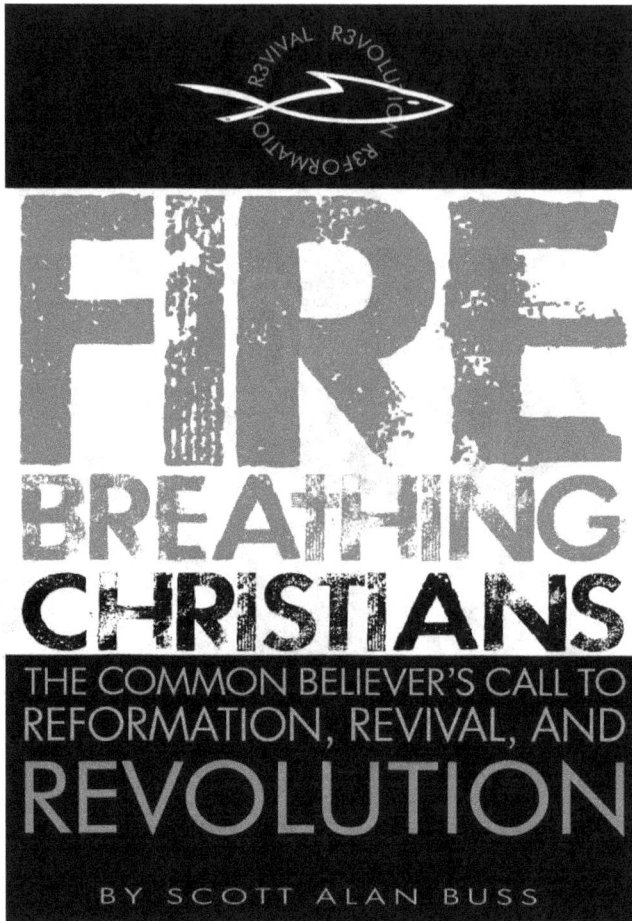

www.FireBreathingChristian.com

the

FIRE-BREATHING CHRISTIAN

PODCAST

HELL RAZING RADIO
www.FireBreathingChristian.com

STiCK PEOPLE FOR JESUS

A Tale of Two Churches

See: Matthew 28:18-20; Matthew 6:9-13; 2 Cor 10:5

See: Matthew 7:13-23; Jude 1:4

For more *Stick People for Jesus* comics, visit
www.FireBreathingChristian.com.